THE
GREEN TRIANGLE

*Being the History of the 2/5th
Battalion The Sherwood Foresters
(Notts & Derby Regiment) in the
Great European War, 1914-1918*

By
W. G. HALL

(The Buffs, sometime attached 2/5th The Sherwood Foresters)

WITH A FOREWORD BY
Brig.-General **T. W. STANSFELD**,
C.M.G., D.S.O.

The Naval & Military Press Ltd

❖

Reproduced by kind permission of the Central Library,
Royal Military Academy, Sandhurst

Published by
The Naval & Military Press Ltd
Unit 10 Ridgewood Industrial Park,
Uckfield, East Sussex,
TN22 5QE England
Tel: +44 (0) 1825 749494
Fax: +44 (0) 1825 765701
www.naval-military-press.com
www.military-genealogy.com
www.militarymaproom.com

TO

THE MEMORY

OF

THOSE WHO DIED

THIS BOOK IS

DEDICATED

" Now, lads, remember you are British, and fight—fight
for England !"

(A small " B " Company Corporal to his men when the 2/5th
Battalion were surrounded at Bullecourt, March 21st, 1918.
He was killed almost immediately afterwards)

PREFACE

THIS History was undertaken at the request of Lt.-Col. C. Herbert-Stepney, D.S.O., Secretary of the Territorial Force Association for the County of Derby.

It records the life and exploits of the 2/5th Battalion Sherwood Foresters from its inception to its finish in the Great European War 1914-1918.

It will, it is hoped,'together with companion volumes written round the doings of sister battalions from Nottinghamshire and Derbyshire, keep alive in a permanent form the part played in Armageddon by the men of these two counties.

It is a record of which any county should be proud.

No attempt has been made here to do more than tell the story of this one Battalion. Neither the wider history of those years with their ebb and flow of success and defeat, elation and despair, to final triumph ; nor the strategical and tactical necessity for movements of large bodies of troops from one area to another, have been touched upon : moves from place to place are given as they occurred without digression into possible reasons. This is just how they appeared to the men : the Machine was on so vast a scale that a small unit like a battalion could, in the nature of things, realize but little of the purpose and plans of the brains directing.

An attempt, however, has been made to treat the theme in as interesting a way as possible. A sincere effort has been made to indicate the atmosphere created and humanized by our lads through so many terrible months.

The wastage and strain of the war were so great that few men, serving with a fighting unit, were lucky enough to remain with the same battalion throughout the war.

vii

This History, therefore, has been built up from the terse Official Diary which every unit had to keep, together with the notes and recollections of a number of officers who served with the 2/5th for varying periods throughout its life. For although it was the author's fortune to be familiar, in time of war, with most of the places mentioned in this book, including Ireland (if not whilst with the Battalion, then whilst with some other), it could never have been undertaken by him but for the generous help and advice of many willing friends. His debt to them is hereby gratefully acknowledged.

His best thanks are due to Lt.-Col. C. Herbert-Stepney, D.S.O., for his never-failing courtesy and readiness to assist in the procuring of relative records, etc. : to Lieut.-Col. J. C. Baines, D.S.O. ; Major R. S. Pratt, M.C.; Major F. E. M. Donne ; Captain H. M. Clifford ; Captain H. Waterhouse ; Captain J. N. Jacques, M.C. ; Captain T. H. L. Stebbing, M.C.; Captain F. Woolley-Smith, D.F.C., for their recollections and notes; to Lieutenant H. C. Heane for his sketch map of the attack on Cologne and Malakoff Farms. Especially is he indebted to Captain C. N. Littleboy, M.C., who has assisted materially with the text, corrected the proofs and checked references. In addition most of the illustrations are from blocks kindly lent by him. Further, his two little books *C Company 2/5th Sherwood Foresters in France*, and *The Battles of the Hundred Days*, have been largely drawn upon and have proved invaluable.

W. G. H.

March, 1920.

CONTENTS

ix

CONTENTS

MAPS AND PLANS

ILLUSTRATIONS

FOREWORD

By Brig.-General T. W. STANSFELD, C.M.G., D.S.O.

*Captain W. G. Hall has asked me to write a Foreword
to his book, " The Green Triangle," which is a history of
the 2/5th Battalion, The Sherwood Foresters. It gives
me the greatest pleasure to try and do so, as I commanded
the 178th (Sherwood Foresters) Brigade from April 6th,
1917, until it was broken up in May, 1918, practically the
whole time it was on the Western Front.*

*I well remember the day I joined the Brigade at Bernes.
In the afternoon I walked up to reconnoitre the line held
by the Brigade, and on the way went into a cellar at Vendelles and there met Lt.-Colonel St. Hill, Commanding the
Battalion. He was rather down on his luck over the failure
of the attack carried out by the Battalion two days previously,
so vividly described in Chapter V of this book. However,
the morale of the Battalion was excellent—it could not have
been otherwise, with such a good lot of officers and N.C.Os.
to lead their men.*

*On May 3rd the Battalion attacked Cologne and Malakoff
farms, and although taking part of their objectives, were
unable to hold them. This was another great disappoint-
ment to all ranks. The men, when they made the attack,
were very tired, having, as far as I remember, been holding
the line up to forty-eight hours before the attack took place.
The attack was to be carried out during the night—always
a hazardous proceeding—and there was little time for
reconnaissance. Moreover, the men had had only one
night in bed previous to the attack. The comparatively
pleasant time spent in the Havrincourt sector was very
abruptly marred by the death of Lt.-Colonel St. Hill. He
was respected and loved by all ranks, and was most human.*

Colonel Gadd came shortly afterwards to take over command. To show what his capabilities were he was specially selected to command the Battalion when he was holding the appointment of General Staff Officer, 3rd Grade. Few officers experienced such quick promotion, and equally few deserved it.

The attack on September 26th, 1917, near Ypres, was most successfully carried out. It has been very accurately described in Chapter VI, which includes Colonel Gadd's clear report on the part taken by the Battalion in this action.

At last the Battalion had taken part in a real success, and in spite of the heavy casualties incurred, all ranks were exceedingly proud of their share in it.

The period spent in the Lens sector was moderately quiet, and no battalion had any chance of distinguishing itself to any degree.

Then came the surprise attack at Cambrai. The success of this attack was entirely due to secrecy. I rejoined the Brigade from leave at Blairville about 2 a.m. on the morning of November 20th. Lt.-Colonel Martin, who was commanding the Brigade in my absence, told me of the impending operations, and I do not think that anyone in the Brigade, with the possible exception of the Brigade-Major and Staff-Captain, had an inkling as to what was going to take place. Ours was the last Division in reserve, and was originally intended to exploit any success beyond Bourlon Wood. The story of Cambrai is well told in this book, so needs no further enlargement. At one time during the enemy counter offensive I had lent the 2/5th, 2/6th, and 2/7th Battalions to other brigades or divisions, and I completely lost touch with the 2/6th for nearly two days. Information during that period was most difficult to get, and one chiefly lived on rumours—but did not rely on them !

Capt. Swann's death at this period was a very great loss to the Battalion. He was a most efficient Company Commander.

The " Petit Garçon " story about Capt. Farnsworth is quite true, but practically in the same paragraph there is

*a description of his rum punches and corpse-revivers, as
if I had concluded my visit by partaking of one of them. I
never had an opportunity of tasting either!*

*One of the best performances in the Brigade Cross
Country Run was that of Capt. Nadin. He was, I think, in
the first three, if he did not actually win it. Anyhow, he
won a good deal of money from one of the Brigade staff over
his performance.*

*The part the Battalion took in the great enemy offensive
on March 21st needs no words from me beyond that I am
certain no battalion fought better on that day than did the
2/5th. Its casualties were enormous, and it had a most
difficult task to perform. Anyhow, the enemy on the Brigade
front only penetrated just over one mile in depth, which
speaks for itself, compared with other parts of the British
front further south.*

*Looking back on events, I am sure we should have done
better if our Sector had been held more lightly, i.e., by one
Battalion occupying the line held by 2/6th and 2/7th, one
Battalion where the 2/5th was and the third in Brigade
reserve. It may be argued that the leading Battalion would
certainly have been overwhelmed if that plan had been
adopted, but it was a recognized fact at that period of the
war that, given sufficient artillery preparation, any system
of trenches could be taken, therefore the fewer men who were
put in that system the better. Depth was the secret of success
both in defence and attack.*

*The Battalion suffered irreparable losses that day,
notably Major Trench, the Padre Judd and Captain Nadin.*

*Major Trench was one of the finest officers it has ever
been my lot to meet. Judd was all that Captain Hall says
of him. Captain Nadin was wounded by a shell at Brigade
Headquarters in the early hours of 21st, and subsequently
died of wounds. He was a most hard-working, conscientious
and cheery officer.*

*The story told of the little Corporal in " B " Company
shows the spirit that was then running through the Battalion.*

*The reorganization of the Brigade took place as described
in Chapter IX. The men composing the drafts were really*

splendid, as although 50 per cent. were boys who were frightfully keen, the remaining 50 per cent. were, in the majority of cases, seasoned soldiers. What we lacked were officers. The quality of the latter could not have been better, but the quantity was negligible. The way the Battalion fought during those most trying seven days at Kemmel, in April, 1918, reflects the highest credit not only on the Battalion as a whole, but also on Lt.-Colonel Baines and his stout officers and N.C.Os. who led them, and their conduct there was a fitting last act in the fighting life of the Battalion, as shortly after, much to everyone's sorrow, the Division was broken up, and it was a sad day when all Battalions marched away from the barracks at St. Omer. If only the authorities who were responsible for the man power question at home could have foreseen the demands that were going to be made on the manhood of the nation, then they could have provided for it, and the Sherwood Forester Brigade would not have been broken up.

A story is quoted of the Americans in Chapter X, which is typical from the little I saw of them. I remember two parties of American officers being attached to the Brigade in the Lens sector. Both parties came and saw me after their tour with companies of the Brigade in the line, and they both made exactly the same remark when leaving, namely: "Wal, General, we've got to thank your men for a lot, and I guess we have something to learn."

It was with the greatest interest that I read Chapter XI, "The Remnant," which gives an account of their doings in the last hundred days under Captain Littleboy and other officers; it must have been a great consolation to him that he was allowed to take over his sister Company in the 5th Battalion and retain some of his N.C.Os. and men who had done him so well in "C" Company of 2/5th.

In conclusion I wish to add what an honour it was for me to have commanded a Brigade during part of the Great War composed of such officers and men as those who filled the ranks of The Sherwood Forester Brigade.

T. W. STANSFELD,

October, 1920.   *Brigadier-General.*

The Green Triangle

CHAPTER I

BEGINNINGS

News of the battle! News of the battle!
Hark! 'tis ringing down the street ;
And the archways and the pavement
Bear the clang of hurrying feet.
—AYTOUN, *Edinburgh after Flodden.*

ON Monday, June 25th, 1914, men opened their news-papers and casually noticed that an Austrian Duke and his wife had been assassinated the previous day some-where on the Continent.

Beyond a passing sympathy for the victims of the outrage English folk were not stirred. It never crossed the minds of the vast majority of them that their own lives, the lives of their family circle and the destiny of their country, were to be profoundly affected by this event. Racial and political jealousies in the Near East were remote from their everyday life and too little under-stood for the full significance of the crime to be apparent.

The murders, as all the world knows, were the work of a crazy Austrian subject of Serbian birth. On this simple fact was built up the *raison d'être* for the War. Had the assassin been of Italian, German, English or Russian nationality there would have been no Great War—then. And in the uttermost corners of the earth men would have gone on with the daily task of living, quite unconscious of the Call that might have come to them to forsake all that they held dear, everything that they had planned, in answer to the need of the Mother-land.

But the " excuse " was taken. In the month that followed secret diplomacy was busy ; there was much

interchange of notes between two great Chancellories.
The Germans saw their opportunity and seized it. Plans
long and carefully matured dealing with the Balkans
and Asia were now to take actual shape, and the most
perfect military machine this world has ever seen was
to put them into force. The quarrel was made. " The
Day " had come.

Yet, at the beginning of August in England the issue
was still in doubt. Men believed that the storm-cloud
would blow over and life go on tranquilly as heretofore.
The community proceeded to spend its Bank Holiday
in the usual fashion. People started off for the seaside ;
lads and lassies in Derby, Nottingham, and Church
Gresley donned their Sunday clothes and their brightest
ribbons and enjoyed the week-end to the full, unconscious of the threatening doom overhanging them. In
London the crowd of trippers on Hampstead Heath was
as great as in former years. Thus England on the eve
of Armageddon.

Meanwhile in Downing Street the Cabinet sat in
continuous session. In Whitehall small groups stood
about discussing the situation and watched the comings
and goings of Ministers.

Towards evening our ultimatum to Germany became
public and English intervention in the conflict certain.

But even then, few, if any, realized in all its stark
totality the far-reaching effects of this decision.

Holiday-makers in merry mood made the news the
occasion for singing and horseplay. Total strangers
linked arms and paraded the streets in bands shouting
the latest comic song or " catch " phrase. Before
Buckingham Palace a huge crowd gathered crying insist-
ently for the King.

Presently the French windows over the great central
archway opened, and the King, the Queen and the Prince
of Wales came out on the balcony and stood. The
crowd immediately hushed itself to silence. The great
arc lamps surrounding the Queen Victoria Memorial
cast long straight beams and shadows upon the thousands

of flushed faces upturned to the balustrade, where stood the King, symbol of Empire and keystone of an Idea, to protect which many there would, on the morrow, die. A woman's voice began " God Save the King " and the vast assembly took it up. The shadowy group on the balcony, chiefly discernible as white patches where shirt-fronts caught the light, silently withdrew. The crowd melted away.

On the following day Great Britain was at war.

In the years to come our descendants will wonder how we adjusted ourselves to the coming of war. Items of common knowledge to us, trivial perhaps in themselves, are, therefore, worth touching upon here in order to set the stage as it were and to indicate the atmosphere of the great drama still fresh and vivid to ourselves.

The first weeks after the declaration of war appeared almost uneventful in Britain. Territorials undergoing their annual training stayed on : the rest were called up. Guards suddenly appeared on railway bridges, round reservoirs and at the entrances to tunnels. Where the gallant little British army had got to nobody knew. The press was silent on the point.

Recruiting offices were busy and thousands were enlisted daily. Shopkeepers in London and the provinces displayed posters exhorting the populace to carry on in the old way ; " Business as usual " became the watchword ; one enterprising salesman exhibited the announcement in deep type " Business as usual during alterations to the map of Europe." Due largely to good British commonsense and, for once in a way, prompt action on the part of the Government in declaring a moratorium, there was no panic. A few unpatriotic persons, with the instinct for self-preservation largely developed, commenced food-hoarding, but the general impression was that the War was too big to last long and would be well over by Christmas. Many months, almost years in fact, were to elapse before a full realization of the effort needed to crush the foe was to dawn on the British public.

B

Newspapers were prodigal in editions. There was, then, no hint of a paper shortage. Every day, stories of thousands of Austrians killed by Russians alternated with stories of the piles of Russians left dead on the field by the Austrians. It is computed that in the first three weeks of the War the whole of the Austrian and three-fourths of the Russian forces were annihilated—by the evening papers.

Meanwhile the hosts in grey in countless numbers, fully equipped with guns of every calibre, poured into Belgium. The Belgian army fought stubbornly and well, but was outclassed at every point.

For the first time in civilized history methodical "frightfulness," based on a scientific theory, true child of German mentality and "kultur" about which the world was soon to learn so much, was introduced towards a civilian population. The stories of open towns and villages sacked and burned, priceless buildings and treasures wantonly destroyed, of the old and the feeble tortured and shot, women and girls raped and innocent children massacred, created astonishment and disbelief among English folk which rapidly gave place to fierce resentment, rage and hatred (as the full horror of the truth became known) against the men who did these things.

Meanwhile, no news of the British Expeditionary Force. "Where is it? Has it come into action yet?" men asked each other, but none, outside official circles, knew. At last the veil of silence was lifted. England learned that its forces had come into touch with the Germans on August 23rd, at a little place called Mons.

Then came the first great call for volunteers. In every newspaper, on every hoarding, on trams and buses, even on the windscreens of cars and taxicabs, flared appeals. Kitchener called for one hundred thousand men, volunteers for service for three years or the duration of the War. Three years? Why the War wouldn't last three months, so worked the minds of people in those seemingly distant days of '14. The rush to the colours was tremendous. High and low answered the Call ; the recruiting depôts were besieged by fellows of all ages eager to join up.

The Youth of the nation suddenly became aware of Adventure—rare and splendid—beckoning to each man personally, and instead of turning in at the familar office or workshop door, they followed where it beckoned and fell into place in the endless queues waiting to sign on. Lads stood in line and discussed with chance neighbours the likelihood of being taken. Vivid must be the memory, to every man lucky enough to survive, of the day he enlisted, marking as it probably did the moment when he first met Jim and Joe, future pals in many a tight and bloody corner. Who at the time could foresee that out of such heterogeneous mobs of fellows, with little in common, except youth and enthusiasm, discipline was to weld a force mighty enough to hold in check and finally to smash the much-vaunted military machine of a great Power ? Who, again, could, looking at them then, have foretold the long drab years, the weary vigils in muddy holes and ditches, through seemingly endless rainy nights, which these pale flabby boys from desk and bench would tenaciously endure and joke withal ? Would the youth of England have been so keen, so eager to " get there " had they known the road ?

And so the appeal for men went forth and the response to the appeal was tremendous. From all parts of the Empire they came, drawn irresistibly by the magnet of race and blood, to the Homeland in its hour of stress.

Each evening lads all over the British Isles went home to break the news of their enlistment to their folk, whilst across the seas steadily ploughed ships bringing ever nearer yet other volunteers. At the same time across the Channel in Northern France, in places soon to be familiar to thousands of English-speaking men, old Jules Dubois was jerking the muck from his boots in the fading light preparatory to going in to his supper, wondering meanwhile how his son Jean fared amid the fortunes of war.

Battalions were formed in a day. Territorial units completed their establishment at a bound. Second (reserve) battalions were authorized and up to strength almost before they officially came into existence. Camps sprang into being everywhere like mushrooms in the night on fields, parks and commons. In the streets, on school playgrounds, anywhere, men, still in civilian clothes, were busy learning to hold themselves properly, to form fours, to submerge their individuality in the group. Others, past their prime, veterans, " sweats " of other days—old army N.C.O.'s in battered straw hats or cloth caps—appearing magically apparently from nowhere, with voices rusty from disuse, took the raw material and began to mould it.

Men were billeted in all sorts of places both likely and unlikely, in barns, stables, cinemas, empty houses and upon the populace ; thousands were billeted at home. Every scrap of canvas was utilized, marquees and tents, thousands of them leaky and rotten and long since condemned, were requisitioned. In places the muddle was terrific. Food supplies went wrong ; the cooking was frequently atrocious. Green fields, pleasant grassy camping grounds, became water-logged wildernesses when churned up by the feet of men and horses in rainy weather. Tents were flooded out or blown down. Men spent days and nights together in wet clothes and wet blankets, nursing aching muscles and blistered feet— entirely through sheer ignorance and inexperience.

But gradually knowledge came in the best way, through hard mistakes. Day by day organization improved, training progressed, muscles hardened and bodies became more and more able to withstand fatigue. Officers began to know their men, to appraise them and to promote the ablest to stripes. The machine was taking shape.

It was amid scenes such as these that the 2/5th Battalion Sherwood Foresters was born and quickly grew like Rabelais through sturdy childhood to lusty youth.

CHAPTER II

TRAINING

RALPH. March fair, my hearts! . . . Open your files, that I may
take a view both of your persons and munitions.—
Sergeant, call a muster.
SERGT. A stand.
RALPH. Let me see your piece, neighbour Greengoose. When
was she shot in?
GREEN. An't like you, master Captain; I made a shot even now,
partly to scour her, and partly for audacity.
RALPH. It should seem so certainly, for her breath is yet in-
flamed. . . . Where's your powder?
GREEN. Here.
RALPH. What—in a paper! . . it craves a martial court.
Where's your horn?
GREEN. An't like you, sir; I was oblivious.
RALPH. Sergeant, take a note on't, for I mean to stop it in the
pay.

—The Knight of the Burning Pestle (1613).

ONE does not look for sentiment in an official record,
yet it is impossible to read the brief and laconic statements in the War Diary of the Battalion now kept at
the Records Office without feeling moved. Of what a
multitude of hopes and fears, toil and trouble, blunders
and triumphs, by frail humanity do these simple entries
speak to one reading between the lines.

" The first men were enlisted under date 5/10/14 at
the following places : Derby, Belper, Swadlincote, Long
Eaton, Ilkeston. Seventy men were attested and pro-
motions of old N.C.O.'s were made." Thus, modestly,
begins the history of the 2/5th Battalion Sherwood
Foresters.

The nucleus, to which this original entry refers, was
made up of old non-commissioned officers, who had been
in the Battalion before and had resigned, and a leaven of

newly-joined recruits.   Every day squad drill was carried
out in the Drill Hall, and the numbers grew as recruits
came along.

Uniforms were not immediately available, but as the
khaki came in men were sent to the Q.M. Stores in batches
of fifty to be fitted.

On the 16th first Battalion Orders were issued by
Lieut.-Colonel Maurice Hunter, T.D., under the heading
" 5th (Home Service) Battalion Notts and Derby Regiment." The Orders were signed by W. R. H. Whiston,
Major and Acting Adjutant.   On the 23rd Orders No. 2
were issued showing men attested and posted to companies.

The following day the Unit left Derby for The Hayes,
Swanwick,* and as men enlisted and were clothed they
were sent on to join the Battalion there.   By the end
of the month the Battalion's strength in other ranks was
about 580 men : 38 men were transferred to the North
Midland Divisional Ammunition Column.

During November men continued to flow in until about
the 15th or 16th, when recruiting was stopped.   A draft
of 120 were transferred to the 1/5th and struck off
strength.

By the 30th the whole of the Battalion was in training
at Swanwick with a strength, exclusive of officers, of 882
N.C.O.'s and men.

Clothing, however, was by no means complete, the
men as yet had no khaki greatcoats and no equipment.
So that any parade in greatcoats, though charming no
doubt from the point of view of infinite variety, was
hardly soldierly in appearance.

The Battalion possessed just enough rifles to go round
the Quarter-guard ; and even then a serious discrepancy
occurred between the number of rifles and the number of
bayonets on charge.   Special words of command had

* In after days Swanwick became the scapegoat for many kit
deficiencies. At The Curragh, when a man was found to be short
of some article of kit, his great excuse always was, " Lost at
Swanwick, sir, in the wash."

to be improvised when changing guard to meet the situation. One order ran " Old-guard hand over bayonet ! "

The Hayes, though not ideal, was a good place for the purpose. It had accommodation for a whole battalion, with good washing and bathing facilities, a dining hall in which half the Battalion could sit down at the same time and a concert hall large enough for company drill in wet weather.

It was during the stay of the Battalion here that *The Subalterns' Guide to Promotion* made its appearance after breakfast one morning. When the rush for copies was over it was discovered by some that they themselves had already supplied a good deal of the matter contained therein. As for instance. Question : " How do junior officers carry their arms on parade ? " Answer : " With the extremities thrust as deeply into the trouser pockets as possible."

The Official Chronicle now becomes dull reading with its continuous reiterations of " The Battalion carried out general training," " The Battalion paraded for a route march," or " A kit inspection was held," enlivened occasionally by such cryptic entries as " Pay Parade," and " ' F ' and ' G ' Companies entertained visitors." As to whom the visitors were that " F " and " G " entertained the Diarist is silent. It has been suggested that this apparently social occasion was really a part of the general training, the visitors being of the multiplying sort, later to be familiar yet uninvited guests in every tour of duty in the trenches. Careful investigation, however, and a love of truth compels us to dismiss this inference as unsound. It is more likely that the time was a festive one dedicated to the amusing of wives and sweethearts who came to see husbands and lovers in their soldier clothes and to glimpse the new and strange conditions under which they were living. This was the lighter side.

Early and late, throughout the short winter days, training went forward at a rapid pace. Squad and rifle drill, musketry practice and route marches, followed each other in quick succession. The gentle art of " belly-flopping " was learned—a species of open-air musical chairs in which men learned empirically to be adjacent to a patch of grass (even if wet) rather than a puddle when the sergeant's whistle sounded the " flop." Training was progressive ; men sought their level everywhere. Duty men began to thin the sections in all directions : cooks, sanitary men, signallers and pioneers went off to their various lairs. Examinations of N.C.O.'s were held by the Commanding Officer. Gradually the Battalion took form and began to realize itself for what it was, a unit complete in itself with its own *esprit de corps* and traditions.

Too, the strenuousness of the régime began to weed out the weaker. The physically unfit man is not only useless to an army, he is a positive burden and nuisance to all concerned. Thirteen men were discharged as medically unsound in the first four months. Four were dismissed the Battalion for " unsatisfactory conduct," an interesting sidelight on the spirit prevailing at that time and the prevalence of men willing to enlist. Battalions could pick and choose their recruits.

A Y.M.C.A. hut was built and opened by the Bishop of Southwell early in December, adding greatly to the comfort of the men. Concerts were frequently held. It was on one of these occasions that an officer, not a young one, was asked by the C.O. to conduct a party of ladies, who had come to give a concert, to the hall. The men had been waiting for some time. On the officer's sudden appearance on the platform closely followed by nine fair females, absolute silence reigned for a moment, quickly followed by the whole room bursting as one man into " Hullo, hullo, I am surprised at you!"

Although recruiting had ceased, men to the number of thirty were enlisted about this time to fill up the gaps left by men discharged or transferred to the 1/5th Battalion.

On January 30th, 1915, to the consternation of company commanders, the double company establishment

was put into operation.   Apart from the army two
classes of civilians benefited by the alteration, the sellers
of books on the new infantry training and the purveyors
of midnight oil.   Officers commanding companies went
about their quarters with faces drawn from much study,
small red books bulging their tunic pockets contrary to
Regulations.

"B" and "E" became No. 1 Company, "A" and "F"
No. 2 Company, "D" and "H" together formed No. 3,
and "C" and "G" made up No. 4 Company.

Four days later the Battalion moved south to Luton.
Having worn straw hats during the summer season for
many years, at last discovering a more becoming type
of head-dress, our soldier boys enjoyed this change to
the home of the straw hat industry.   The War was still
fresh enough to ensure them a ready welcome and their
dialect a passing interest.

A few days later a further, but only temporary, move
was made to Broxbourne and Hoddesdon in order to
obtain entrenching practice, the men returning to billets
at Luton at the end of a fortnight just in time to catch
the postman dumping 963 Japanese rifles and ammunition upon a long-suffering and inoffensive Quartermaster.

O, that Rifle, Japanese Mark goodness-knows-what,
with its ramrod, numerous little tools and cleaning
gadgets, to say nothing of the quaint little leather
walking-out belt, with the strip of untanned leather
inset that accompanied it!   For what blasphemies and
worry it was responsible.

March opened with the arrival of a draft of a hundred
men from the depôt.   On the 3rd, General Sir Ian
Hamilton, G.O.C.-in-chief, inspected the Battalion.

During this month Imperial Service volunteers were
asked for and an Imperial Service Company was formed.
But it was not till June that the Battalion became definitely a Service Unit.   On June 7th, a date that may be
said to be its real birthday, the Battalion moved by
road with the rest of the Brigade into camp at Dunstable
under the command of Captain F. E. M. Donne, the Home

Service officers and men remaining in Luton being formed into a Provisional Battalion. Seven days later Lieut.-Colonel G. C. Aitchison arrived and assumed command. At the same time Colonel Maconchy, C.S.I., took command of the Brigade.

Meanwhile training continued and was, if anything, more intensive than ever. Much repetition makes perfect. Long hours in the open air and hard work began to have its reward and to show results in the assured, upright, alert carriage of the men ; in their brown faces and clear eyes. A month at Dunstable, and on the Battalion went again, with heavy packs and bulging haversacks, taking the dusty road to Watford, coming finally to rest in tents amid the leafy trees of Cassiobury Park, the property of the Earl of Essex.

It is only human to have prejudices, and Tommy is always very human. Each of the many towns and villages, in which it pleased a kindly War Office to station the Battalion for any length of time, had its champions among the men. Mostly such preferences were based on the remembrance of a kindly billet, a pretty chance acquaintance of the opposite sex, or, even, on the quality of the ale sold at the local hostelries. But there they were. At every place some men were found who were loth to leave behind them another landmark on their journey towards France. Of all the towns touched at, Watford, probably, holds the first place in the affections of the largest number ; memories of the days spent there lingered vividly in the minds of the boys when overseas in the after years. Jokes and stories commencing " When we were at Watford " enlivened many a chat round the stove in the billet or the brazier in the dug-out. Why Watford took such a hold on the imagination of the men it is not difficult to see. Here for the first time came realization to the fellows that they *were* a Service Battalion near the end of their training and destined at any moment for the real thing " over there." The pleasant little frills of ordinary life take to themselves fresh beauty and attractiveness the nearer the danger of losing them becomes. Coupled with this there is no doubt that the good folk of Watford were more than hospitable and kind to all soldiers. Many battalions passed through Watford and all of them, without exception, looked back with pleasure to their stay there.

The month of September saw the arrival of little amenities like travelling field kitchens, pack saddlery, etc., items which go to the full equipment of a unit in the field. Knowing ones cocked an eye and said, "Now we shan't be long before we're off." Frequent inspections by the Staff helped to lend colour to this view. It was just as if Brass Tabs No. 1 had said casually to B.T.'s No. 2, "Oh, by the way, coming thro' Watford the other day I ran across quite a smart turnout in battalions. You might run down and look them over : they may be one of the lost regiments. Have a glance at the ' mislaid ' list before you go." So Tabs No. 2 came along and inspected us, went back, told his friends, and they in turn came along and had a look at us. However that may be, inspections became the order of the day. The first line transport, arms and equipment, were inspected on various occasions by the Brigade Commander. The G.O.C. 59th (N.M.) Division inspected the Battalion and again on October 1st, in company with the rest of the Brigade, the Battalion marched to Gorhambury Park, St. Albans, and were inspected by General Sir Leslie Rundle.

Inspections are a weariness to the flesh of all concerned. Everyone realizes their necessity and the excellent effects of the work and discipline involved ; the *esprit de corps* engendered. It does men good to see their battalion or their brigade at its best, splendid to the last buckle and button, alert and watchful that no mistakes occur to detract from the honour of their corps.

But nobody gets violently excited when they hear that a promised inspection is " off," or looks forward to one with any degree of enthusiasm.

The stages in an inspection are progressive and to the

lay mind highly involved. The atmosphere, cloudy and heated in the lower strata, becomes rarer and rarer and positively pure in the higher altitudes. If the General has notified his intention of inspecting you at 10 a.m., the game, really played properly, starts occasionally as early as 7.30 or 8 o'clock when the corporal throws a friendly eye over his section. He is closely followed by the platoon sergeant whose eagle glance misses nothing, each man finding himself pushed and pulled into shape—straps tucked in and an already perfect pack squared a bit more. Next on the list comes the platoon commander, and yet more adjusting takes place. "Jones'" pack is too low, and "Smith's" belt too loose. At this juncture approaches the company commander, closely followed by a hot and perspiring company Q.M. sergeant, showing in every line of him the marks of a hard driven and embittered soul. O.C. company has firmly made up his mind before he arrives that its the worst turn-out he has ever seen. Not a single man is correct. Proceeding on this assumption he soon has his complacent platoon commanders by the ears, the sergeants almost weeping and the symmetry of the files temporarily marred by the number of men who have been " fallen out " to continue their struggles with recalcitrant straps or equipment. Eventually the company commander, outwardly resigned, but secretly highly satisfied and proud, marches his company to the battalion parade ground. Once again the men looking straight to their front undergo the keen scrutiny. This time the inquisitor is the commanding officer. He seems apparently most casual and aloof as he passes up and down the ranks. But it is only an illusion ; he misses nothing. In close attendance upon him comes the platoon commander, the O.C. company, the adjutant and perhaps the senior major, then the regimental-sergeant-major, the company-sergeant-major, and the company-quartermaster-sergeant.

The colonel mounts his horse, and with the band leading, their instruments and trappings shining in the sunlight, the battalion marches to the forming-up ground.   On

arrival dust is flicked from boots and puttees, markers
are set, ranks opened and dressed, officers take posts.
An interval of waiting ensues. The men stand easy, but
are warned not to move and so lose their dressing.
The last cautionary words are whispered—" attention "
called as the brigadier rides into the field accompanied
by the brigade-major. He rides slowly round, yet one
degree more aloof and cool than the colonel. Another
wait. The men are allowed to stand easy but not to
talk. The hour approaches and instinctively, to the
latest-joined recruit, we get ready. Down the road in a
swirl of dust, punctually to time, come one, two, grey
military cars at high speed, and the General followed by
his staff strolls slowly towards us. The General Salute
is sounded. " Tompkins " in the rear rank of the first
platoon of " B " Company fumbles and finally drops his
rifle. O.C. " B " Company breaks out into a cold sweat,
but thank Heaven no one outside " B " Company appears
to have noticed it.

" Officers, non-commissioned officers and men of the
2/5th Sherwood Foresters, I am very pleased and proud
. . ." The General is speaking. He has used the same or
similar words many times before, and we have heard
before, or will hear again, the same or similar phrases
either from him or another G.O.C., but we are none the
less pleased and gratified to hear our secret pride in our
regiment endorsed. Finally we march past and swing
away down the road for home with rifles slung and fags
and pipes in full blast. We know ourselves for a splendid
lot of fellows and our battalion for the best in the army.
We have been on our feet in full marching order for over
four hours and feel we could stick it a good deal longer.
All the same we're not sorry its over.

Very wild weather was experienced about this time,
and training was to a certain extent interfered with.
The Battalion was vaccinated, which still further interfered with parades. Inoculations had been carried out
earlier in the year.

The last three months of 1915 were taken up mainly

by Divisional field operations, places like Serches Farm,
Whitehouse Farm and Serches Hill being attacked or
defended with equal warmth and according to orders.

Trenches dug in Moor Park were held and night reliefs
carried out without casualties. Full advantage, too,
was taken of the local miniature range. Bombing
practice became a part of the weekly routine. Bombs
lost their terrors, and their playful habits thoroughly
known. Following the procedure of the Israelites of old
when dealing with the Ark, small tins filled with earth to
represent bombs were almost daily " pitched without the
camp."

On October 18th, camp was struck and officers and
men moved into the luxury of billets. Yet, in spite of
the softness that comes to men who live comfortably in
houses, the Battalion was able on the 26th to take up a
defensive position in Black Boy Wood and hold it
successfully against determined assaults from the 2/8th.

On the last day of the month church parade was held
in the Central Hall, and the address was given by the
Rt. Rev. The Lord Bishop of Southwell.

After the style of " Old Moore " November may be
said to have opened unluckily for " D " Company, who
were ousted from their billets and had to be content with
the spartan simplicity of Parkgate Road School. On the
10th, bayonet fighting, musketry, close and extended
order drill and physical exercises were carried out in
Callowland before Major-General Dickson (Inspector of
Infantry).

During December the system of sleeping in large
empty buildings was adopted throughout the Battalion,
and the companies moved in turn into their new area.

Towards the close of the year special leave was granted
the men, 10 per cent. of the establishment proceeding
on leave at five-day intervals. As a crowning act of the
year, and to everybody's great relief, Japanese rifles
were handed into store.

On January 2nd, the Battalion was inspected on a
route march by the G.O.C. 3rd Army, otherwise the New

Year opened without much change in the, now so familiar, routine. Men came back off leave and settled down with greater or less ease according to temperament, but settle down they did to the daily round and common task. A large number of recruits, amounting to more than two hundred and fifty men, joined the Unit during this month. These were all trained together and were eventually inspected by the G.O.C. Division on the 22nd, and again by General Sir Alfred Codrington, G.O.C. 3rd Army, during the second week in March.

During March, too, 700 Rifles, M.L.E. Mark III* Short, were received, besides four Lewis-guns, and everybody felt that the apparently long postponed trip overseas must at last be near at hand.

A new form of torture lent additional colour to this view. Practice moves became frequent. The alarm would be given and the men would pack furiously, only to find at the end of it all that it was a wash-out. Privates on nodding terms with the Orderly Room Sergeant, and therefore in the know, would whisper confidential tit-bits to their pals and the pals would go to bed in their boots and equipment, haversack bulging with canteen produce, feeling they were at least one up on the uninitiated. Usually their secret information proved fallacious, to the great undoing of the prophets. But who ever heard of a prophet having honour in his own battalion ?

Occasionally the Germans came to the assistance of these minor diviners of events, and when the aircraft alarm sounded, their credulous followers had some satisfaction in the realization that they, at least, were ready.

But although " wolf " was cried frequently during these early months the moment was rapidly approaching when the word was to be shouted to some purpose. The Battalion was at last to sally forth upon active service, but to a land and against a people they little dreamed.

CHAPTER III

IRELAND

KEEGAN : Ireland, Sir, for good or evil, is like no other place
         under Heaven, and no man can touch its sod or
         breathe its air without becoming better or worse.
                —G. B. SHAW, *John Bull's other Island*, Act IV.

THE War Diary, extremely attenuated as it is for the
years 1914-15, becomes almost shadowy for 1916.

Nineteen-sixteen is the year of the Irish Rebellion,
against which the Battalion took a part, and it is regrettable that a fuller account of the happenings of this time
has not survived. The Official Record stops abruptly
at May 30th, and even then the month of February is
missing altogether. An ordinary reader can peruse the
whole of this year's Diary in under five minutes.

Therefore, in the following account of our Battalion's
life and adventures in Ireland, it has been necessary to
rely almost exclusively upon the memory of those who
were present in the Unit for the whole, or a portion, of the
time. Great care has been taken by those to whom I am
indebted for data and anecdotes incorporated here that
their recollections should be as accurate as it is possible
to make them. Soldiers on active service usually
discover it a somewhat unsafe proceeding to keep a diary,
and few, of the very few who did, found either the time
or the inclination to keep a very full one. If, then, in
the story of this year small inaccuracies do occur, they
will be found, I hope, to be merely negligible and not
likely to detract from the book as an authentic record.

Towards Easter, then, just as everyone was beginning
to fume at the seeming inactivity in England—with its
daily monotonous drudgery of musketry practice and

drills in Cassiobury Park and field days at Radlett,
nine miles away—orders were received to hand in barrack
stores, preparatory to a move to Salisbury Plain to be
finally fitted for France. The Battalion, ever prompt in
the carrying out of orders, began to obey, when a further
despatch was received, "move postponed."

So life went on peaceably as heretofore, and at Easter
leave was granted in the usual way, everybody being
due back on the Monday night.

At 7 o'clock on this evening, April 24th, instructions
were suddenly received to be ready to move, followed,
four hours later, by definite orders.

Practically none of the men who had been given leave
were back, and, of those who had been unlucky enough
not to get leave, few were in billets. Officers and men
were scattered, as officers and men usually are after
parade hours, *chacun à son goût*; some at the theatre,
many at the various picture palaces, pubs and other
places of amusement and relaxation in which Watford is
rich, not excluding those who found their pleasure in
Cassiobury Park strolling (not alone) beneath the gnarled
old hollow trees that there abound.

But news of this kind soon gets round, and the men
began to find their way back to billets to prepare. At
the theatre an announcement was made, and at every
picture palace the news was flashed upon the screen,
" All men of the 178th Brigade will return to quarters,"
causing quite a flutter which, for the nonce, placed
Charlie Chaplin a very bad second.

" Another sanguinary alarm," men said to each other
as they said good-night to their girls and hurried back to
billets. But they were wrong. The move was a real
one this time, but where nobody could guess ; surely it
couldn't be France at such short notice, and if not to
France, then, by all that's holy, where ?

During the night preparations went forward, and before
day broke the Battalion had marched to the station and
entrained. Appeals to the guard and engine driver, who
should know where their train is going if anybody should,

c

threw little light on the mystery. The guard suspected
the destination to be Liverpool, but didn't know. Just
as the train moved out the 2/6th Battalion could be
seen approaching the station on the same errand.

The suspicion of the guard was correct, and the
Battalion eventually detrained at Liverpool Docks and
immediately began to shift the transport, horses and
stores aboard the packet steamer *Munster*.

Here the consciousness that they were *en route* to
Ireland dawned upon the Battalion. The steward of the
boat had just crossed from Dublin and the pretty stories
he retailed lost nothing in telling—that is, *nothing*
dramatically, whatever they lost in veracity. Sinn
Feiners had seized the Post Office, and other public
buildings, and had practically taken possession of the
entire city. British officers had been shot.

The *Munster* steamed away from Liverpool as dusk
was falling, bad sailors noting with pleasure a smooth sea,
and nervous men, with relief, the accompanying des-
troyers. Kingstown Harbour was safely reached by midnight and disembarkation commenced immediately. As
soon as they had landed, "C" Company were detailed for
duty at Arklow, started straight away, and the Battalion
did not see them again for two months. The 2/6th
Battalion arrived soon after, and when the unloading of
both boats was completed the two Units marched away
from the town, through barricaded and guarded roads,
slogging steadily on for quite six miles up hills steep
enough to compete with any to be found in Derbyshire.
Eventually the guide led the Battalions off the road into
a small park-like enclosure fronting a large house. When
daylight came this proved to be a Roman Catholic
charity school. The surprise of the children at seeing
two thousand men in their grounds, arrived apparently
from nowhere, was humorous to watch ; but they very
soon made friends with the fellows. The night had been
spent without cover and an early breakfast proved welcome.

News came by despatch rider from Kingstown that the

2/7th and 2/8th, together with Brigade Headquarters, had landed there and were about to advance on Dublin through Black Rock; the 2/5th and 2/6th were to advance parallel to them along the Stillorgan-Donnybrook road.

With a solemnity and caution almost humorous the march began. The 2/6th with a party of cyclists threw out an advance guard, and slowly, with halts and starts and halts again, the column gradually neared its objective. It was during this journey that the Padre dilated at length to his neighbours on the many and varied methods employed by him to defeat foot-weariness : on the different powders he carried for this purpose in his haversack and how he prepared his socks. His was, in fact, one of those heart to heart talks that in the after months would have delighted the soul of Major Trench.

The people in the Dublin suburbs turned out *en masse* to greet the Brigade. From all sides offerings of oranges, bananas, sandwiches and chocolate, were pressed on the men. Women walked beside the battalions holding the saucers whilst our overwhelmed Tommies hastily gulped down cups of tea. Meanwhile on the Black Rock road the 2/7th and 2/8th were meeting with a very different reception. They encountered considerable opposition and suffered regrettable casualties. Our column was heading straight for College Green, where the Sinn Feiners were reported to be fortified, when a despatch rider arrived with fresh orders, and in obedience thereto the Battalion swung to the left by Harcourt St. station and proceeded by the North Circular road to the Kilmainham hospital. Footsore and weary, but without incident, they reached the hospital about 5 o'clock.

Kilmainham hospital stands on a high hill and looks down on to Kingsbridge station and the river Liffey. From the direction of Island Bridge came the sharp pong of a field gun, and the new arrivals looking down suddenly saw a round hole appear in the side of a tall square house standing apart beside the river. A burst of rifle fire followed and the observers could see brick-dust and splinters flying from round the windows marking the places where the bullets struck.

The men spent the night in the huge armour room whilst most of the officers slept as comfortably as they could in the pews of the beautiful little hospital chapel.

The following day a few picked stout-hearts under the direction of gigantic Sergeant Cunningham cautiously approached and searched two houses near Kingsbridge station, from which it was surmised shots fired at the Royal Irish Constabulary Headquarters had come ; but without incident. If either house had contained any Sinn Feiners they had long since made good their escape by the back door.

The next day the Battalion sent a detachment of three officers and eighty-five other ranks to Island Bridge barracks as a garrison, and also took over the guard at the station. Here a most heterogeneous collection of officers from many regiments was found. Returning from leave they had been held up by the stoppage of the trains. Battalion Headquarters made itself thoroughly at home in the directors' room, and quite excellent quarters were found for everybody about the station premises. The refreshment-room had been untouched by the rebellion, and it was unanimously agreed that it would be a pity not to make use of its contents.

The complex system of outposts elaborated by Captain Stebbing for the proper protection of the sheds, sidings and the line where it crossed Island Bridge and entered the tunnel under Phœnix Park was the wonder of all beholders, and many were the anxious moments spent by " A " Company officers trying not to be shot in the back by their own sentries.

On the whole the time spent at Kingsbridge was without event. The sentries at the front entrances to the station were sniped at on several occasions and once or twice had an opportunity of replying. Otherwise the time hung rather heavily. A certain amount of excitement was to be got watching snipers of some of the Irish regiments, working outside the station from points of vantage among the chimney-pots, in their efforts to catch the unwary.

Sackville street was in flames and burning fiercely. The progress of the fire could be followed from the station roof.

One day the sentry at the main entrance saw a most villainous looking ruffian coming towards him along the deserted street. He was covered, challenged, the guard turned out and the man arrested. Standing over six feet, dressed in rags, a red muffler round his throat and with four days' growth of beard on his face, the guard felt they had indeed made a capture. On being taken before the Colonel the prisoner's identity was disclosed as that of an officer of a Lancer regiment, quartered at the Curragh, out for information. This officer was afterwards pounced upon by a party of Sinn Feiners as he was passing the Four Courts and held prisoner by them. He eventually got away two days later by declaring himself to be a newspaper reporter out for copy.

By the 29th, the City was comparatively calm. Occasional sniping continued, but it was isolated and sporadic. The order to cease fire was received at 4.30 p.m. The military had rapidly gained the upper hand. A cordon had been drawn round the disaffected area and field-guns brought into action soon destroyed any houses in which Sinn Feiners were holding out. Rounding up began and hundreds of prisoners were taken. Our men saw many batches go past the station on their way to Kilmainham gaol. In one batch, conspicuous in green breeches, tunic and enormous broad-brimmed hat complete with ostrich feather, was the Countess Markeovitch.

During these days in Dublin the Battalion had a comparatively easy part to play. Not for them were sensational captures, charges down Sackville street or skirmishes on College Green, though all these excitements fell to the lot of the rest of the Brigade.

At the beginning of May, though, it took its share of cordon duty and the enforcement of martial law, guarding barricades and patrolling the fetid alleyways in the appalling slums that are such a terrible disgrace to the City of Dublin.

On the 5th, the Battalion left the station and took up its residence in Guinness' brewery in James street, but to the lasting regret of those whose darling ambition always is to be right amongst "it," Brigade thought forty-eight hours quite sufficiently long in so ideal a billet and moved the Battalion back to Kilmainham hospital, thus relieving a detachment of dismounted cavalry.

About this time the first line transport arrived, as did also personal kits. The officers and men left behind in the hurried move from Watford also rejoined.

Prisoners were now being sent to England in large numbers and the Battalion was called upon on three separate occasions to supply the escort.

On May 16th, the Battalion moved into camp in Phœnix Park. The Park was at its best at this time, the trees and shrubs beautiful in their early summer freshness; the landscape vivid with that translucent vividness seemingly only to be found in Ireland.

Messing arrangements were, however, somewhat primitive. The officers' mess consisted of a footboard from an ablution bench mounted on S.A.A. boxes, other S.A.A. boxes forming the seats. It was here, too, that the Adjutant (always something of an epicure) made his famous confession of taste. Looking at his plate he remarked, in a hoarse voice tense with feeling, that " he did not mind it high and he did not mind it tough, but he was damned if he liked it raw." Apparently the cooking became suddenly as primitive as the furniture.

On the 23rd, eighty-three recruits arrived from Derby and were inspected by the G.O.C. Division on the 26th.

The following day " B " Company proceeded by route march with Brigade Headquarters to the Curragh, the remainder of the Battalion following the next day under the command of Captain Nadin, the Adjutant, both the Colonel and the Second in Command being detained on a G.C.M. in Dublin. The first night was spent at Rathcoole, the second at Naas, the Curragh being reached on the 30th.

It was on this march that the Battalion enlisted another recruit at the unusual charge of 2s. 6d. He was very young—still a kid, in fact—and was soon known throughout the companies as Billy. Owing to his age Billy was committed to the care of one man who tended him and taught him how to deport himself in the world. The antics and playful attacks of his childhood were harmless and amusing, but when he became older and stronger and his horns were sharp his butts were no joke. He was adopted as the Battalion mascot.

Later when the Battalion left Ireland, transportation of Billy became a problem. Unauthorized animals were not allowed. However, Billy duly answered the roll-call at Hurdcott, thanks to the initiative of Drummers Hemsley and Whitehouse, who smuggled him thither in a sack. On the journey Billy was so unsporting as to bleat frequently and at wrong moments for milk. A retinue of pals had to be kept near at hand constantly on the alert to drown all such manifestations by loud coughs and sneezes. When the Battalion moved overseas it was found impracticable to take him along, and he had to be left behind to the tender care of the Australians.

Everybody was pleased to get away from Dublin ; the weeks spent there had not been weeks anyone had enjoyed. Actual war is not a pleasant game ever, but it usually has the advantage of being straightforward in one particular anyway, namely, that one's foe can be recognized on sight by his clothes. But in Dublin, with both the friendly portion of the population and the rebellious dressed mostly alike, it was impossible to tell them apart. Many stories are related showing the difficulties frequently in the way of those attempting to track down snipers for instance, but one, perhaps, will suffice to illustrate. The military were much harassed by rifle shots coming from the direction of a certain house. The house was surrounded and entered. The only occupant found therein was an old woman who stoutly denied that any firing had taken place from her place. The house was searched and a rifle newly-fired was found in her bed. She then confessed that she was the sniper.

Incidents such as this filled our simple Derbyshire boys with amazement. Why, their own womenfolk in their home villages would be physically incapable of even firing at a foreign invader, much less at their own people. They simply could not understand why they should be so fiercely hated by folk speaking the same language and to whom they had, as far as they knew, done no harm.

The difference in the reception accorded to the two halves of the Brigade, in their approach to Dublin by separate routes, emphasizes this existence of the friendly and the unfriendly side by side and was observable all through. Set in an atmosphere purely Irish it was at one and the same time both pathetic and humorous, turning the Rebellion on occasion into farce. Our fellows had frequently to ask assurance from each other as to whether they really were awake or merely taking part in a realistic dream.

A British officer walked into the G.P.O. and calmly asked for a penny stamp long after it was in Sinn Fein hands. Irish boys looted a sports shop in Sackville street and played golf in the main roads with bullets whistling along it. Another authenticated story tells of an old woman who dashed into a shop after loot, brought out an armful and asked a policeman to look after it whilst she went in for more. Sinn Feiners used to taxi home from the barricades for food, returning again by taxi to the scene of the fight. A little later in November a poster was displayed broadcast, apparently without hindrance: "Conscription. All true Irishmen will oppose this. They can best do so by joining the National Irish Volunteers." The mere statement of this sentiment in England at that time would have met with heavy penalties.

The majority of our men had never heard the words Sinn Fein until they found themselves at Liverpool. Many knew in a hazy sort of way that the Irish were

always kicking up a row and were never satisfied, but
they never realized the height and depth of hatred of
most Irishmen to everything English until they set foot
in Ireland.

At the Hippodrome, at the close of the performance
each evening, *God Save the King* was invariably hissed
by the gallery and pit and also by a few in the circle and
stalls.

A group of Irish children were seen standing in front
of a shop window amusing themselves by systematically
spitting in turn at each picture postcard exhibited of
soldiers and sailors.

It is, of course, impossible here to enter into the causes
which make the Irish problem so complex. But a
brief word is perhaps necessary in order to explain why,
in the midst of a great world war, it came about that our
Brigade, which was so badly needed in France, had to be
sent west at short notice instead of east. The Sinn
Fein Movement was originally an intellectual, non-
political body. It confined its attention to the keeping
alive of the Irish Language and the Irish National Spirit.
Irish poetry has always been rich in a charm of imagery
and spiritual beauty all its own, surpassing even the
Celtic passion and form of the Welsh. This the Sinn
Feiners fostered.   Stories of grievances, real or imagined,
tyrannies suffered, families driven overseas to foreign
lands by the hated Saxon, were told generation after
generation to the children ; they grew up with the knowledge of their country's wrongs firmly fixed in their
minds, and a burning hatred of all things English in their
hearts.   To a people in temper such as this, Sinn Fein,
emphasizing as it did their mighty past, gave spiritual
fire and idealism to their cause.

That is why every Sinn Feiner who was condemned
to death stood in the courtyard at Kilmainham before
the firing-squad, drawn from a sister Battalion to our
own, steadily, like men, without flinching, and without
support.   All faced the rifles not as craven rebels, but
like men dying for a great Idea.   Soldiers who were

present, ever susceptible to courage whenever they find
it, acknowledge this.

But to return to the Curragh.

Curragh camp is situated on undulating downland
in the centre of the county, 3½ miles east of Kildare
town. The camp was established in 1855 with accommodation for 12,000 troops. The Curragh itself is
also famous for its race-course.

As the 2/5th Battalion spent six months or so on this
undulating down, a little fuller description will not be
out of place.

The Curragh is about thirty miles south-west of
Dublin, and the downs are about six miles long by two
miles wide. To reach the Curragh, the traveller has to
go by train from Kingsbridge station to Newbridge or
Kildare and then walk or go by jaunting-car to the camp.
It was always a mystery why no railway—not even a
light one—had been built from Kildare or Newbridge to
deal with all the military traffic to and from the camp.
But the jarvies said, " If there is a railway we will lose
our business ; therefore no railway shall be built."

Curragh camp consists mainly of barracks—quaint
old white-washed ones, more modern ones built of red
brick, and still later ones of tin (for the duration of the
war). There is also a theatre, a gymnasium, a post
office, a few shops, an abattoir or slaughter-house, a
water-tower, and last, but by no means least, " Sandes'
Home "—a species of Y.M.C.A.—by day the resort of
the "light" and "excused-duty" men, and by night the
meeting-place of many in the Battalion.

When the Battalion first arrived at the Curragh, it
went into tents at Hare Park camp, just to the west of
the barracks, but on July 11th it moved into a tin-hut
camp five-hundred yards or so further away from the
village. This camp was well laid out. The huts surrounded on three sides the parade-ground ; on the west
were the officers' lines ; on the south, the Battalion
orderly room, and on the east the company lines,
arranged in five rows running east and west. As regards

the company lines, starting from the north, first came "A" Company, then "B" Company, then the mess-huts, kitchen and baths, and lastly "C" and "D" Companies.

Just to the west of the camp is the Gibbet Rath—a stronghold of early prehistoric times. Here in the summer evenings men would sit and watch the sun setting, talking the while about leave, Luton and Watford, and then about Watford, Luton and leave—three inexhaustible topics.

In the boiling days of summer the Curragh was a splendid place, but what a change autumn and winter wrought—came rain that turned the lines into a sea of mud, and bitter south-west winds that swept across the downs and once (so the legend goes) uplifted a hut from the officers' lines and deposited it on the parade-ground where the occupants found themselves, much to their astonishment, when they awoke in the morning.

In each draughty hut there was a stove, but in the majority of cases no chimney or only its rusted remains. In the whole camp there were scarcely twenty good chimneys and with the coming of winter these changed hands most nights. If you had a chimney one night, you could " bet your ' bally hat ' " you would not have one in the morning unless you were very much on the alert and awake all night. To make up for this chimney shortage, home-made ones, manufactured from tins of all sizes and shapes, were used. These were all right with the wind in the right quarter, but when the wind came, as it usually did, from one of the many wrong quarters, the contents of the chimneys blew back into the huts. It was not till December that new chimneys arrived for all and men could sleep in peace in sure knowledge of a chimney still in place in the morning.

It was said that if a human being lived through a winter at the Curragh, he could live anywhere—and as the Battalion found itself the following winter still living, *and* quite happily, in worse places than *anywhere*, the saying was probably true.

The Battalion, with the readiness which is such a

characteristic of life in the army, returned to the *status quo ante*, Dublin, without much effort.   Ordinary routine parades recommenced interspersed with field manœuvres. For although the Battalion was a Mobile Column ready to move anywhere at a moment's notice, it (unlike the 2/8th, which departed suddenly for Athlone) was never called upon and spent the remainder of the year in much the same way as it spent its time in England, keeping itself fit and learning each day yet a little more about the art of war.

For the remainder of this chapter, therefore, a tedious repetition of training parades carried out will be as much as possible avoided : these the reader will understand went forward in the usual way, side by side with cricket, football and other forms of sport, so much a feature in the life of the Battalion at this period.

The 2/5th was under strength in company commanders and seconds in command.   Any expectations the senior subalterns may have entertained in this direction, however, were suddenly dashed when, at the end of June, without warning, five captains swooped down on the Battalion from the D.L.I., and they came with rumours of an immediate move to France and active service, their swords as keen as razor-blades from much sharpening. These five from the " Faithful Durhams " were posted as follows : Captain P. E. Adams to command "B" Company; Captain C. N. Littleboy to "C" Company, as 2nd in command; Captain R. S. Pratt to "A" Company, as 2nd in command; Captain W. Swann to " D " Company, as 2nd in command ; and Captain S. M. Wadham to " B " Company, as 2nd in command.   The last-named officer was with the Unit only a short time, however ; a previous application by him for a transfer to a Wireless Section came through soon after he joined.

Captain Wadham was the last to arrive (on July 11th) and reached the Battalion when it was in the midst of the move from the canvas camp at Hare Park to the tintown under the shadow of the Rath. (They were taking over the huts from the 2/8th Battalion who were off to

Athlone to stop some playful cattle-driving the Sinn
Feiners had just begun). Naturally Captain Wadham
thought that this was the move to France of which he
had heard rumours and said to the C.O. on reporting :
" Just in time I see, sir." But the Colonel soon dis-
illusioned him by saying that they were only moving to
the tin camp five hundred yards away. As some sort
of consolation, Captain Wadham was detailed to carry
out the assessment of barrack damages in the 2/8th
camp before the Battalion took possession. Thither he
repaired and found a Quartermaster awaiting him. With
" I suppose you were waiting to go round the huts " he
introduced himself. Together the two went round the
camp, arguing every hole in the asbestos lining, every
cracked pane of glass, every missing chimney. At last it
was done and Mr. Farnsworth said, " Come and have tea
with me." Then and not till then, when they found
themselves walking to one and the same mess (their own),
did they realize that they both belonged to the same
battalion. They had spent two tedious hours in vain!

At the beginning of July the General Musketry Course
was in full swing on the Little Curragh and Curragh
ranges. Naturally there was keen competition between
battalions. The 2/6th in particular were supposed to
be desperately keen on being top scorers. The story
went that the Commanding Officer of a certain unit made
any man in his battalion who fired on a wrong target
stand up and shout, " I am a damned fool, I've fired on
another man's target."

The Battalion had not been at the Curragh long before
a cricket pitch had been made and rolled and nets erected.
These latter were pitched just outside the officers' mess
to the great danger of its windows, as a lofted late cut to
third man or an erratic ball from some vigorous bowler
used to thud against its wooden walls.

The cricket XI had among its number some good men,
one Derby County player (Major R. B. Rickman) and
two Derbyshire " colts " (C.Q.M.S. H. Wild and Sergeant
W. Reader-Blackton). Then, too, there was Captain

Wadham of googlie fame and Pte. J. H. Green with his slow swerving left-hand bowling. The tail of the team though was poor, but it wagged sometimes with fair success.

Of the many matches played one of the most exciting was the Right-half Battalion v. the Left-half Battalion on July 22nd—a boiling day. This match ended in a tie, the finish being most dramatic. "A" and "B" Companies batted first and compiled a total of 104 runs. "C" and "D" Companies had scored 104 when their last man went in. The first ball sent down was a half-volley and the batsman took a mighty swipe, hitting the ball fair and square amidst the cheers of the Left-half—the winning hit they fondly imagined. But Captain Adams at mid-on put out his left hand—felt something hit it—looked—and saw the ball. Quietly and unobserved, for all eyes were on the boundary, he threw it to the bowler. He had a bruised hand for weeks, but he had saved the match.

Rumours of the Division being about to proceed to France continued prevalent, and the Divisional staff decided that before going abroad the artillery must have some practice. With unusual promptitude the C.R.A. managed to procure a few shells, to the intense delight of the gunners.

Such an occasion as this could not be allowed to pass without the poor infantry being once more pressed into service, and a Divisional circular announced that an artillery field-practice and demonstration with live shells would take place in the Wicklow Mountains in which the infantry would co-operate and practise attacking under barrage-fire. Needless to say, the infantry looked forward to these opeiations with less enthusiasm than the gunners.

Two companies from each of the 2/5th, 2/6th, and 2/8th Battalions Sherwood Foresters had to be selected for this enterprise. From the 2/5th Battalion "B" and "D" Companies were chosen, and on a sweltering morning (July 29th) paraded at 8 a.m. and, commanded by Major R. B. Rickman, set off on their twenty-mile march, each with the inevitable pick or shovel and full pack, and accompanied by a small transport column with blankets and cookers.

The march was performed in two days, a halt for the night being made at Dunlavin, where all slept in the open in a field near the village. Parading early the next morning, the march was continued, and in the afternoon the destination (a beautiful spot in the valley of Glen Imaal at the foot of the mountains) was reached.

Here all were accommodated in tents, and a Sandes' Home being in the vicinity, all looked forward to a pleasant week ; a welcome change from the Curragh surroundings.

The R.F.A. had already arrived and directed the work. This consisted of digging assembly trenches and erecting marks and barbed wire as targets for the artillery.

The weather was perfect and the mountain air invigorating, and soon all were burnt almost black by the sun. The work proceeded so well that by the end of a week a very considerable system of trenches had been completed and all was ready for the practice attack.

Early on the morning fixed for the practice the gunners were asked to register their guns in the clear light of dawn, and much chaffing was heard amongst the infantry concerning short shooting and lost messages.

Soon the Divisional staff and representatives from units in the Division arrived, followed by General Sir John Maxwell, Chief of the Irish Command, with part of his staff from Dublin, and the show commenced.

The infantry first practised occupying their assembly positions and were then withdrawn to a safe spot (in case of accidents). The gunners now had their turn, and after a few rounds of slow fire, to represent a " standing " barrage, quickened the rate of fire and lifted into a creeping barrage which gradually died away in the distance. The infantry again took up their assembly positions, and the barrage being represented by men waving coloured flags, assaulted, captured, and consolidated the enemy position.

The field-day ended with a short talk to all the officers by Sir John Maxwell.

Next day the return march to the Curragh commenced and Dunlavin again forming a halting place, the troops reached camp the following afternoon.

The Brigade, except the recruits, having completed its musketry two months previously, Division decided that field-firing should now be carried out on a large scale, whole companies, even, firing at once, if possible. For this practice Glen Imaal was again selected, and each battalion in the Brigade ordered to proceed there for a week in turn.

The 2/5th Battalion was allotted the first week and, leaving all the recruits and a few instructors under the command of Lieutenant Binks in camp, set off on August 18th with full transport for the Wicklow Mountains.

The advance guard was provided by No. 1 Platoon, (2nd Lieutenant D. Wright) and the baggage guard by No. 16 Platoon, (2nd Lieutenant Lavender). The route lay across the Curragh from the camp to the Low Curragh road, by Jockey Hall, Old Kilcullen, Gormanstown to Dunlavin. The day was hot, the roads narrow and dusty, and the hedges, as usual in Ireland, high and untrimmed, so that several extra halts were necessary. During one of these the advance guard lost touch and completely disappeared.   Nor was it discovered for fully two hours, when it emerged from a by-road full on to the head of the column, to its own astonishment and the indignation of the Colonel.

Dunlavin is a queer old, typically Irish, country town with straggling uneven streets, a rickety town hall, police barracks, pretty girls, many public-houses and a barber's shop.   The latter was particularly noticed because of the following curious notice displayed in its window : " We always try to please our customers who are expected to help us.   Gentlemen are requested to wash their faces at home before coming to be shaved." After passing through the village, the Battalion climbed the long steep hill and turned into a field on the right of

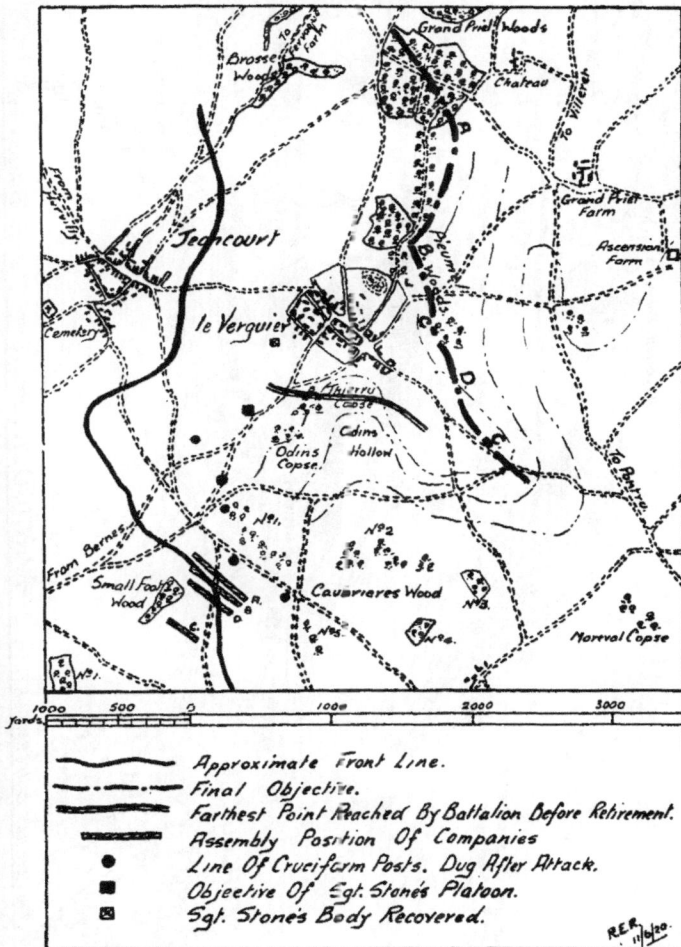

The Attack On Le Verguier.
4th April 1917

Legend:
~~~~~~ Approximate Front Line.
—·—·— Final Objective.
▬▬▬▬ Farthest Point Reached By Battalion Before Retirement.
▬▬▬▬ Assembly Position Of Companies
● Line Of Cruciform Posts. Dug After Attack.
■ Objective Of Sgt. Stone's Platoon.
⊠ Sgt. Stone's Body Recovered.

R.E.R. 11/6/20.

[See Chapter V

MALAKOFF AND COLOGNE FARMS. 4/5/17. SKETCH MAP.

[See Chapter V

the road. A wheel—at the halt on the left form mass
—pile arms —take off equipment — fall out—and the
Battalion as one man sat down with a sigh of relief.

This was the halting place for the night. A welcome
meal from the cookers was served, feet washed in a
neighbouring stream and inspected, and blankets drawn
from the transport. Company lines were allotted and
bivouacs of ground sheet and blankets erected. These
were the only shelter, but fortunately the night was fine
though somewhat chilly.

In the small hours of the morning the C.O., poking his
head from his temporary bivvy, spied a large party of
grimy cooks in the next field busily engaged in milking
a number of cows and collecting the milk in mess tins.
His roar not only startled the cooks, but effectively
wakened the whole Battalion, while the R.S.M.'s batman,
mess tin in hand, was seen to fade quickly away from the
neighbourhood of the cows. Rumour said that the C.O.
in his anger gave the order for the milk to be put back at
once, but this is believed to be calumny.

After a hasty breakfast the march was continued.
Donard, a pretty little village shut away among the foot-
hills, was passed, and then the scenery became wilder,
hedges giving place to stone walls as the mountains were
approached. The well-marked conical hill, the Sugar
Loaf, with its steep screes, was kept on the left as the
Battalion swung down and entered the valley of Glen
Imaal and proceeded to the camping ground amongst the
pine trees and bracken.

Scarcely had tents been drawn and pitched when
shouts of excitement denoted that rabbit hunting had
commenced. The men, armed with sticks, stones and
entrenching-tool helves, surrounded a patch of bracken
while beaters entered and drove out the rabbits. The
produce of the hunt went to the company cookers and for
days the companies feasted royally.

The first three days were fine and warm, and many
bathed in a deep pool in the mountain stream. After
this, however, the weather broke, squalls of wind and

D

rain soaked everything and the camp became a quagmire. Shooting took place daily, and many collective practices obtained excellent results and a great deal was learnt.

Rain was so heavy and persistent that no one was sorry when end of the week saw the Battalion on its return march to the Curragh. Dunlavin again formed a resting place for the night, but a soaking blanket and a pool of water forming no inducement for delay, the march was resumed at dawn the following morning, and by midday the troops, soaked to the skin and tired out, were back in their huts.

The following day volunteers for a draft for overseas were suddenly called for.

No Battalion likes parting with its men and although all service battalions, whose luck it was to remain in England for any length of time, went through the experience of sending many of its best men to France as drafts to other units, use never made the occasion anything but a sorrowful one. The 2/5th was no exception to this feeling. Of all the drafts that left the Unit that which left this September from the Curragh was felt the keenest. The men had been with the Battalion so long and the hope of going out with their friends so certain to all concerned.

August 27th was indeed a sad day for the Battalion. Just before breakfast, during early morning parade, the company commanders were told that each company had to prepare a draft of fifty N.C.O.'s and men for immediate service abroad. Also rumours were rife that the whole Battalion would be sent out in drafts by September 9th, and preparations were to be made accordingly. With one fell blow all hopes of service overseas as a battalion were squashed. Soon, however, another rumour spread abroad—it was said that Sir John Maxwell, Commander-in-Chief in Ireland, had wired the War Office saying, " Cannot be responsible for Ireland if 59th Division broken up." Be that as it may the order for preparing the remainder of the Battalion for draft was washed-out, though the order for the draft of 200 N.C.O.'s and men, unfortunately, held good.

So it was in no cheery mood that each company saw many of its best men volunteering for service, made up their kits, filled in their various army forms, and signed their pay books.

At 6 p.m. on September 2nd, the two hundred men were assembled in one of the dining-halls while the Battalion gave them food, drink, and cigarettes. Then at 9.15 p.m. the draft were paraded, and amidst cheers from the pals they were leaving and with the band at their head (Mr. Farnsworth performing ably on the big drum) they marched away under the command of Major Donne to Kildare railway station and service overseas.

A few days later took place what, in the after days, was humorously referred to in the Battalion as the Battle of the Sods.

On September 7th the usual parades, Brigade bombing classes, outpost and attack schemes, P.T. and B.F., Lewis-gun classes, etc., were cancelled and the Battalion was warned for a big attack practice at the Brigade training area near Killcullen. The actual name of the Brigade training area no one ever rightly knew. On all the ordnance maps the name was blurred. The commonest solution to the puzzle spelt it Moteenanion.

At 4 p.m. the Battalion (wearing fighting order with greatcoats *en banderole*) left the hut encampment and struck off across the Curragh to the French Furze-Brownstown road and then along it towards Killcullen. When quite near this village, the Battalion turned into a field bordering the road, formed up in mass, ground arms, " off-ed " equipment, and were told that no further move would take place till midnight : it was then about 6 p.m.

The last few minutes of daylight were used for collecting dry wood, and soon over the field were scattered little camp-fires, round which men were grouped, talking and eating a " mess " from the field-kitchens. Then, huddled together for warmth, the Battalion dozed the time away till the scheme began.

With whispered words of command, shortly before midnight the Battalion fell-in and moved off at platoon intervals to man the trenches in the training area from which they were to make the assault at 8 a.m. By 3 a.m., without any untoward incident, the trenches were reached. It was a fine starlit night, bitterly cold; greatcoats had been dumped on the way up, and everybody longed for zero hour. Some tried to sleep in the bottom of the trench or propped against the sides.

The system of trenches consisted of a front line, support line and C.Ts. They were shallow in places and deep in others, very irregular and partly fallen in, but very like those in which one day the Battalion would have to fight. In France, though (occasionally), shelters and dug-outs were found, but here there were none except those that had been previously rigged up by the signallers for their own exclusive use.

The enemy trenches had been dug for demonstration purposes by the R.Es.—perfect trenches, well rivetted, with dug-outs, berms and M.G. posts complete. The 2/5th never saw such trenches in France except near the Base.

And this is how the great sod fight began. As day dawned Pte X, boi ed (and frozen) stiff, longed for some amusement whereby he could quicken his circulation and beguile the tedious hours before zero. Looking around he spied over a traverse the head of his old pal Pte. Y. Deftly he shot a small sod and scored a direct hit. Pte. Y quickly returned the shot, but missing the mark hit someone else full in the face. " What the ― ―" that worthy began. The grinning face of his assailant twenty yards away invited reprisals, and a lump of earth went on its unerring flight. Pte. Y called for reinforcements and so did Pte. X, and a right royal battle began. At first the fight was confined to the trenches, but before long the operation changed to open warfare in No Man's Land, and the sky was black with hurtling sods. So the battle went on with varying success until an armistice was called, and the combatants, now thoroughly warmed up, returned to trenches and awaited zero hour for the real attack.

At a few minutes to 8 o'clock a few guns in the distance fired some blank and then at 8 a.m. the Battalion leapt up on to the parapet and the advance began ; but it was all very tame after the other affair.

Soon after 9 a.m., when the objectives had been captured, cease-fire was blown and platoons made a bee-line across broken country to the field-kitchens, where tomatoes and bacon sated craving appetites. Thus ended the Battle of the Sods. No casualties.

As summer waned and the autumn set in, all parades and schemes passed into insignificance before the inter-company football competition, open to the three battalions of the 178th Brigade stationed at the Curragh. As "C" Company of the 2/5th Battalion won the cup presented by the Brigadier (General Maconchy), after a most exciting finish, reference must be made to the competition.

Each Company in the 2/5th, 2/6th and 2/8th Battalions (the 2/7th were away at Fermoy) had to play each other twice, and the company that secured the greatest number of points was the winner ; a win counting 2 points, a draw 1, and a defeat 0. The interest, enthusiasm and rivalry between companies and battalions was tremendous ; in all messes and huts football became the perennial topic of conversation.

"A" Company, or "The Tony Reds," fancied themselves an easy winner—and they might have won, too, if they had only started their victorious career a little earlier in the season. "B" Company, or "The Scarlet Runners," had enthusiastic supporters and finished fairly high on the list. "C" Company, or "The Half Moon Battery," were a really fine team, but even with them there were times, during matches, when faces of partisans on the touch-line went white with anxiety. "D" Company—they assumed no *nom de guerre*—unfortunately suffered from a lack of good players, but they took their defeats in sporting fashion.

As the last phases of the competition were reached, the excitement grew more tense—every item of gossip was thought to bear in some way on the coming matches, as the following true conversation bears witness :

C.Q.M.S. (to A. N. Other when news of the move of the Battalion to England was first announced): " The right-half is going on Tuesday."

A. N. Other : " Oh! Crumbs! Where's he off to—on a course ? Who shall we play in his place ? "

C.Q.M.S. : " No! No!! Not 5181 Harrison, E.—I mean the right-half *Battalion* ! "

A. N. Other : " Thank Heavens! You did give me a turn though."

" C " Company played their last match on January 3rd, 1917, beating "C" Company of the 2/8th. All now turned on the final match between " B " Company of the 2/6th and " D " Company of the 2/8th. This, after the most exciting match ever witnessed, ended in a draw. "C" Company was thus placed securely at the top of the list, and the Cup was presented to them on January 9th.

When the last match had been played " C " Company had shot 77 goals and had 22 goals scored against them, which speaks well for Sergeant R. Hart, the goalie. Of the 77 goals, Sergeant W. Reader-Blackton accounted for 21, Pte. J. H. Green for 14 (nearly all from the left touch-line) and Pte. E. C. Webster for 13.

Concurrently with these inter-company matches there was also the knock-out competition for the Divisional Cup. But the Battalion did not shine in this. It beat the Divisional Cyclist Company 3-0 in the 1st round, but struck a snag in the 2nd round when the R.E. Signals won 1-0.

But to return to the war.

The M.L.E. Mark III* they knew and the Jap they knew, but never in their wildest dreams did they expect to handle and learn to know the Enfield Pattern, 1914, ˙303 inch, magazine rifle, which was a cross between the two.

One day in the autumn, the luckless Q.M. was issued

with these new pattern rifles to the strength of the Battalion. It was not long before he had shot them on to the company-quartermaster-sergeants and the latter had passed them on to the men. It was a tedious, filthy job, removing the thick oil and grease with which they were covered. At last it was done, and the men saw what they looked like and began to learn all about them. The chief points of difference between these new rifles and the Mark III were the aperture sights, the Jap-like bolt, the five-round magazine which, when empty, sprang up and prevented the bolt from being pushed forward, and a longer barrel.

Once more on all sides was heard the low murmur of the " primary extraction " creed. " On raising the bolt lever the bolt is rotated to the left . . ." and that is perhaps as far as many ever remembered.

Then as suddenly as they came, they went. Men smothered themselves and the rifles in grease and handed them in, drawing in lieu thereof the M.L.E. Mark III* again. But, alas! each man's pet rifle, the vagaries of which he had learnt during the G.M.C. and which had become his best friend, was in other hands, and he had to content himself with one that had obviously belonged to one of the "employed."

During the early winter Brigade route-marches were frequent as part of the training. These were of varying length but never less than fifteen miles nor rarely more than twenty. These treks in full marching order, with extra bandolier, blanket and pick or shovel, were carried through with remarkably few casualties as regards sore feet. They also made the men wonderfully fit, and a twelve-mile march was soon regarded as merely a country stroll.

By these marches the Battalion saw a little more of County Kildare than it otherwise might have done. The Irish houses, or rather hovels, in the last stages of dilapidation, the ubiquitous donkey pulling a heavy—too heavy—load, and the vast stretches of unclaimed bog were all new and strange. One of these weekly marches took the Brigade along the raised road that runs through the centre of King's Bog, to the south of Kildare. The measured tread of the column moving down it set the roadway heaving and swinging in a truly fantastic fashion, a revelation to those unacquainted with the phenomenon.

Towards the end of September news came that the Battalion was about to be made up to full strength, and on October 5th, 160 other ranks arrived, followed in two days' time by another draft of sixty. They were nearly all Londoners, and had been called up under the Military Service Act. Amongst them was a Conscientious Objector. He was posted to "D" Company, but "D" Company saw but little of him, as he politely but flatly refused to obey orders and also to wear khaki. Consequently he spent his leisure hours in the guard room and finally left the Battalion to serve a term of imprisonment.

By this time the Yorkshire lads, who had joined the Battalion in the summer, were fully-fledged soldiers, and recruit drills for them were things of the past. They were the smartest soldiers at drill on the Curragh and could knock spots off most demonstration platoons. But instructors were given no rest, and now the Londoners were handed over to their tender mercies. Once more the Curragh re-echoed to loud words of command. C.S.M. J. H. Tomlinson was in charge of the recruit parade and his " Hoolt! Ri——Dre' " was heard from one end of the downs to the other.

In November, Field-Marshal Sir John French signified his intention to inspect the Curragh garrison. Immediately all ordinary parades and training were dispensed with and for the nonce everybody lived in an atmosphere of Blanco and polish.

The review was to be held on the level ground on the north side of the Curragh barracks, and by 8 a.m. units of all descriptions, many from outlying districts, began to arrive. The area had been previously flagged so that there was little difficulty in forming up.

Few there had seen a really big review, and the assembly

of so large a body of troops comprising such various arms
of the service was a most impressive sight.

The Field-Marshal, accompanied by General Maxwell
and staff, took up his position at the foot of the Curragh
commandant's garden, facing the troops. Many ladies
were present to witness the ceremony, their dresses
forming a gay patch of colour as background to the
inspecting officers.

About 10.30 a.m., soon after the General Salute, the
march past commenced, led by the cavalry with mounted
bands, followed by the gunners, cyclists and infantry,
each battalion of the latter with its regimental transport.

After the ceremony, while the troops returned to camp,
the Field-Marshal interviewed commanding officers and
expressed himself as highly pleased with the discipline,
smartness and general turn-out of the parade.

The year finished in an orgy of work. Brigade decreed
that each company in turn should undergo intensive
training. Employed men viewed the order with horror :
transport men feared for their horses if groomed and fed
by those not so skilled in the art ; sanitary men depre-
cated the havoc that would be wrought by untutored
hands ; cooks and storemen groaned at the anguishing
thought of the unsavoury dinners and badly mashed tea
that the Battalion would have to endure in consequence.

But all difficulties were overcome—in turn the men
were relieved from the various employments as their
company started its monthly training. "B" Company
started off with great zeal at the beginning of October,
followed in a month's time by "D" Company. When "C"
Company's turn came along at the beginning of December,
six inches of snow on a frost-bound ground made close-
order drill and schemes almost impracticable. But there
were many substitutes to pass the time away—a run down
to the sewage pond for a slide, followed by an inter-
platoon snowball fight ; also, whisper it, there was the
football field to be cleared for to-morrow's match——
At the end of the month it was found that "C" Company
had not had an opportunity to practise wire-entangle-

ments and the like. A day or two's thaw gave the platoons their chance, and they took it. When "C" Company was inspected on January 4th, by the Brigadier, they passed with honours—much to the other companies' astonishment.

"A" Company, the last to undergo the training, had but little time to evolve and practise their elaborate programme, for they had but barely begun when their training was cancelled owing to the Division leaving Ireland.

But we progress too fast. There was one more occasion which must be dwelt upon before we leave Ireland. The Christmas of 1916 was the last the Battalion was to spend this side of the English Channel, and, unfortunately, for many a lad the last he was to spend anywhere.

Snow in the early part of December raised hopes of a Christmas of the good old-fashioned kind. But no such luck!—a few days before the 25th, the frost broke, the snow melted and the camp was plunged once more into a sea of mud. Christmas Day was quite warm with a dull lead-coloured sky.

Festivities began at 1 p.m. when the Battalion were given their Christmas feed—a sumptuous banquet— turkeys, plum puddings, fruit, beer, lemonade and every sort of vegetable, all were on the menu . . . "C" and "D" Companies were hard at it with knife and fork when Os.C. "A" and "B" Companies rushed into the hall and accused Os.C. "C" and "D" Companies of pinching more than their share of turkeys. "C" and "D" stoutly denied the charge and Major Donne was called upon to arbitrate. The Sergeant-Cook on being interviewed said he had no more turkeys—he had just emptied the last oven. A heated altercation ensued and finally, to make certain, the ovens (of which there were many) were again searched, and lo ! in the end two were twenty frizzling turkeys done to the last turn. " A " and " B " carried them off in high glee, leaving one or two for some still hungry warriors in " C " and " D."

The repast over, the men staggered out of the hall to

take a few minutes siesta before the next event—the officers v. sergeants football match at 3 p.m. Meanwhile the officers and sergeants who had done all the carving and waiting went to their respective messes—the latter to eat their Christmas dinner.

Soon after 3 p.m. the opposing teams were on the field, R.S.M. E. C. Cope blew the whistle and the match began. It was not good football, but it was good fun. The mainstay of the officers' team were 2/Lt. P. P. Harrison at centre-half, and Lieutenant Chandler, a dashing outside right, and undoubtedly the star turn of the sergeants' was the Sergeant Shoemaker, who nipped around the large feet and the long legs of the opposing backs, Captains Pratt and Littleboy. After a most thrilling match, and although they were labouring under a great disadvantage —they had just put away their Christmas dinner—the sergeants won 3-1.

After tea the Battalion adjourned to one of the dining-halls for a concert. Many songs were sung by various performers, but the song remembered best was by the R.S.M., which had a refrain about somebody treading " on the tail of me coite." After the songs and a con-juring display by Private H. S. White came the *pièce de resistance*—a play by Captains Adams and Nadin. The scene was a bit of the Boche front line somewhere in France. In the trench appeared two Germans (Capt. Adams and Nadin) who talked in guttural broken-Eng-lish. Soon the conversation turned to a rumour they had just heard : A Division in Ireland was about to come to France. In that Division was a very fine battalion (doubtless Storm-truppen) called the 2/5th Sherwood Foresters—" and ze rations zey eat! I was told ze best egsample of zere rationing vas ze Quartermaster and ze R.S.M. Zen in ze battalion is a leetle boy but sechs feet hoh. Vat i's ze Engleesh race gomin' to ? Vat, if all ze battalion is like him, vill happen ? Zat is vat I is ask. . . ." So the conversation went on. Though tired and aching from laughter all were heartily sorry when the little play came to an end.

With the play the men's festivities were over except for what amusement might be found in Sandes' Home, but the officers had their turkey and pudding to eat. Afterwards in accordance with old custom in the service they went to the sergeants' mess, where a "ryghte merrie Christmas" drew to a close.

Boxing-Night was notable for the first appearance on any stage of the " Crumps," the 59th Divisional Concert Party.   During the two following years on many occasions overseas our men were to be taken out of themselves by the clean fun and hilarious and never-failing humour of the members of this pierrot troupe.   But although the entertainments given later were undoubtedly, and quite naturally, an advance on this, their maiden effort, few will forget the mirth-provoking programme that accompanied their first concert.

But few copies of the programme appear to exist and those who possess them value them highly.   The present writer has been fortunate enough to borrow one on the strict understanding that it is returned intact at an early date.   The programme is a four-leaved affair.   The front and back are decorated with pen and ink sketches by Sydney R. Jones, all exceedingly well done.   Those on the back purport to be life-like photographs of the members of the Party in characteristic attitudes.   The advertisements which occupy the margin round the items are a pure joy.   Here are a few of them.

Ozone!   Ozone!   Ozone!
Try the cheerful Curragh,
Ireland's Premier Health Resort.

*   *   *   *   *

Cures Hams, Chilblains, Wheezy pianos, Tendency to oversleep, Rotten Poker Hands and Route Marches.

In case of panic : stack chairs ; form fours ; avoid crowding the exits.

EMERGENCY EXIT.

In case of fire or panic cut round the dotted line.

```
┌─────────────────────┐   ┌──────────────────────┐
│      TSCHCH!        │   │   Are your calves    │
│  For snivels try    │   │                      │
│      Tschch         │   │   too small for      │
│  turns sneezes      │   │                      │
│   into smiles.      │   │   your puttees ?     │
│   ──────            │   │                      │
│     S'nice.         │   │     WADHAM.          │
└─────────────────────┘   └──────────────────────┘

┌─────────────────────┐   ┌──────────────────────┐
│     WANTED!         │   │     WIGGLES.         │
│      ─────          │   │       ───            │
│ a strong one-legged │   │  Patent protected    │
│ man to make hops    │   │      POTATO          │
│  for Brewery.       │   │ You cannot cut their skins. │
│                     │   │   12 refills     1s. │
└─────────────────────┘   └──────────────────────┘
```

Thus ended Christmas and the old year, as all years should, to the accompaniment of hearty laughter, good feeling and fellowship. So too, at the same time, ended the stay of the Battalion in Ireland. At the beginning of the New Year orders arrived for the Division to move to Hurdcott. Now Hurdcott is on Salisbury Plain : and Salisbury Plain the ante-chamber to an active participation in the War.

After more than two years spent in England and in Ireland amid rumours and false alarms, the Battalion at long last was about to take its share in the life of dangers, hardships and glory " over there."

CHAPTER IV

I will go where I am wanted, where there's room for one or two,
And the men are none too many for the work there is to do ;
Where the Standing Line wears thinner and the drooping dead
    lie thick ;
And the Enemies of England they shall see me and be sick.
                                —HOUSMAN, *A Shropshire Lad.*

SALISBURY PLAIN is well described as the ante-chamber to war. Most Divisions gravitated there sooner or later. But whether the journey thither was direct or by a slow circuitous route, everyone knew once they had arrived there that their next move would be overseas. Its near and ready access to Southampton and the sea ; its wide unpopulated moors, where troops could be mobilized and easily moved in mass ; and its comparative remoteness from civilization and all that word connotes in the way of temptations to men under orders for the front, all combined to make Salisbury Plain an ideal military base.

The Battalion now found itself in a hutted camp at Hurdcott, three miles from Dinton, very similar in many respects to the one it had just vacated in Ireland. The subsoil here was very chalky, and previous battalions, taking advantage of the fact had, by removing the turf, thrown up their various crests upon the grass-covered ridges. The Royal Warwickshire Regiment, the London Regiment, the Rifle Brigade, the Australian Corps (a kangaroo), the R.A.M.C. and last the V.A.D. badge were all there. A recent order, " That this practice must cease," as it lessened the grazing area for sheep, prevented the Notts and Jocks from adding their own crest to the gallery.

The old fairly leisurely days, with their ample oppor-

48

tunity for healthful sports, now became a thing of the past.
The Division had barely a month to prepare and there
was much necessary detail to complete.

Company commanders and quartermaster-sergeants
had the worst time. It is computed by one O.C. company, with a more than ordinary head for facts and
figures, that he signed his name well over 700 times
during these final preparations.

Extra vests and pants, P.H. helmets, goggles, field-
dressings, tin-hats, wire-cutters, wrist-hooks for bombers,
folding-saws, binoculars and a host of other paraphernalia
had to be served out to the long-suffering rank and file.

In the midst of it all embarkation leave began and the
lists of men who were present and the lists of those who
were not, when this or that prime necessary to modern
war was distributed, reached monumental dimensions.
Happy the orderly room staff which kept its head and
smiled during this trying period.

On February 14th, the Division was inspected in
review-order by the King. A Division, a complete
fighting unit as it is in every particular, is an inspiring
sight when seen drawn up in some natural amphitheatre
on Salisbury Plain. The thousands of infantrymen,
behind them their first line transport, engineers with
their pontoons, signalling sections, field artillery, com-
missariat and ammunition columns are there seen as a
whole, and some idea gained as to the vast complexity
of the machine necessary at the present day for war.

Two days later the frost, which had been almost continuous since the beginning of December, broke, the
air grew warmer, and with a change in the wind came
rain, turning the camp into one vast mud-pie through
which everybody had to wade.

The issue of Hazebrouck and the famous Lens II
maps seemed to indicate the Battalion's probable destination. But the War Office is far more subtle than many
credit, and the officers had ample time to lose both these
sheets before they reached localities in which either of
them would have been of any service to them.

The transfer of the 59th Division to France really began on February 13th, when all battalions were ordered to send advance parties consisting of five officers and ten N.C.O.'s. These were attached to the 50th Division and later rejoined their battalions, those from the 2/5th at any rate, at La Motte, near Warfusée. The Battalion was warned to be ready to move on the 23rd, but on the 20th the move was postponed forty-eight hours.

At 1 a.m. on the 24th the transport, plus a few details under Major R. B. Rickman, left for France via Southampton and Le Havre, joining up again at Vers.

Major G. H. St. Hill arrived this same day and took over command of the Battalion from Lieutenant-Colonel G. C. Aitchison whose age forbade active service.

When on the following morning Colonel St. Hill issued his first orders, headed "Move Orders" and commencing " The Battalion will move overseas to-day (Sunday)," all realized that the moment expected for nearly two-and-a-half years had at last arrived.

At 8.45 p.m. "A," "B," and 110 of "C" Company, paraded ready to move to Fovant railhead, followed at 10 p.m. by the remainder of "C" Company and whole of "D" Company. The march to the station seemed unending. The night was muggy and inclined to rain, and the troops perspiring under heavy loads were glad when the final halt was made at the station.

The two trains left Fovant more or less to time and reached Shorncliffe at 4.45 a.m. and 6 a.m. respectively after a cold and cheerless journey. Here the Battalion sleepily detrained and marched along to Folkestone, where the officers found their way to the Hotel Metropôle while the men were billeted in some empty houses fitted out as a rest camp.

Orders to embark about 9 a.m. were expected, but the authorities were kind and allowed the men to eat their dinner in peace in sure knowledge that it would not be wasted—the sea was calm.

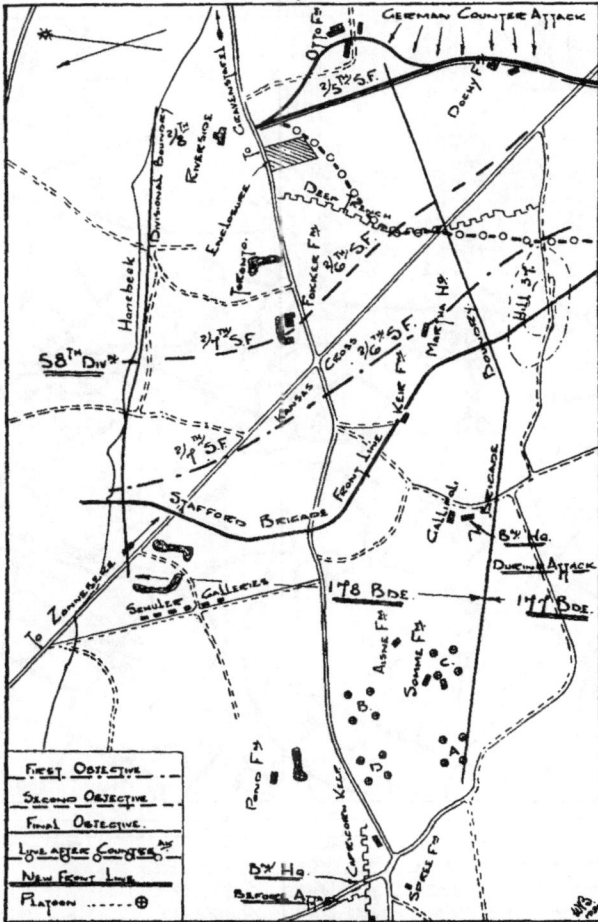

THE ATTACK EAST OF YPRES —
26TH SEPT. 1917.

[See Chapter VI

The fighting around Mt. Kemmel.
April 1918.

Scale.

1000   500   0   1000   2000   3000   4000

_____ Line at 11.a.m. April 13th
_._._._._._._ Line at 6.p.m. April 14th
_ _ _ _ _ _ _ Line at 9.a.m. April 15th
_.._.._.._.._ Line at dawn on April 16th

[See Chapter IX

CHAPTER V

OVERSEAS

. . . . the greatest army which ever at any time of the world's history has crossed an ocean, and far the greatest which a British General has commanded in the field.
—Sir A. Conan Doyle, *The Great Boer War*.

At 5 p.m. on February 26th, 1917, the Battalion reached Boulogne and disembarked. Among the usual crowd of Tommies, R.T.Os., A.M.L.Os., French porters and *gendarmes* lining the quay as the ship sidled in and was berthed, astonished Foresters saw the familiar faces of their Quartermaster, Medical Officer, and Lieutenant Prince. They had been with the Battalion at Folkestone that noon and here they were on the landing stage with the blasé expression of men " out since '14." The explanation (there usually is one) was that these officers by a series of mischances had, to their horror, missed the boat, told their troubles to a patient R.T.O. and had crossed by the fast staff leave-boat which arrived some little while before the Battalion.

Few ever forget their sensations when stepping for the first time on foreign soil. Certainly no soldier living is likely to forget his first impressions of France in time of war. It is one thing to step ashore dressed much like any other individual in Europe ; it is quite another to arrive in a distinctive uniform advertising to all your nationality and the cause which brings you there. To most of the men this was their first experience of travel outside the British Isles and they found it all so very novel and exciting that not even the long march up that extraordinarily steep hill to the rest camp at Oestrohove could appreciably dim. The weather had been wet and the tents appeared to rear themselves forlornly at regular

51

intervals in a vast sea of mud.   To add to the troubles of
a tiring day the second P.H. helmet had to be handed in
and iron rations distributed.   It was midnight before
companies got down to it.

It is probable that Sergeant Morton and the cooks got
no sleep that night, for punctually at 4.30 a.m. breakfast
was served and at 6 a.m. the Battalion was on parade.
The downhill march to the station in the freshness of the
early morning was more pleasant than the same route in
reverse the previous evening.   The men took readily to
the capacious French wagon about which they had heard
so much.   Almost instinctively they began to develop
that preference for the roof of the truck so common
among troops and so difficult to repress.

The train went slowly enough for the dullest-witted to
take in all that he might want to in the way of scenery.
And little children, each on his recognized pitch along the
way, set up their perennial chant for " penny," " bully
bif," or " bisquey."

To those whose first visit to France this was, this
journey up the line was full of novelty.   Everywhere
there were things new and strange.   The railway stations
with their low platforms looked gaunt and bare and the
lettering over the various offices formed words strange to
most.   The railway carriages (many in the last stages of
dilapidation) were known and well understood, but
trucks labelled *Hommes* 40, *Chevaux* (*en long*) 8, what
were they doing in a passenger train ?   The many level-
crossings, with barriers hinged to lift upwards, tended by
women ; the long, straight roads, with their rows of
poplars fading away in dim perspective ; the miles of
huts and huge canvas towns passed between Camiers and
Etaples, with here and there a British cemetery, the dead
laid close together in rectangular blocks, each grave
marked with a little wooden cross—were things all new
and strange. One was off-stage, as it were, and glimpsed
the enormous work going on behind the scenes.

But interesting as all this was, it was as nothing to
the amazement caused by the appearance of the perma-

nent way. For miles and miles the partly grass-grown railway track was littered and strewn with empty tins of all sorts and shapes, cast there by thousands of Tommies as they went up and came down : big round apricot or pineapple tins, oval ones of pilchards, Nestlé's and Ideal tins with two holes pierced in one end, and, most common of all, bully-beef tins, squat, square, with lids half torn off.

At about 5 in the afternoon, much against Mr. Williamson's expressed views,* the Battalion was detrained at Saleux, and had to march in full order to Vers, where, luckily, it found pretty good billets.

The journey had not been completed without a casualty. "D" Company lost Shandy. During one of the many stops, Shandy jumped off the train, whether for exercise or with felonious intent to desert, will never be known. But anyway when the train jolted on again, Shandy was missing and was never seen again. Poor little black Shandy. He had been picked up in Ireland and was devoted to "D" Company men and ignored everyone else. Perhaps it was his devotion to Nellie, Captain Adams' spaniel bitch which had been left in England, that made him sever his connection with the company and attempt, in his doggy way, to return to his love. Who knows ?

The following morning was spent in lazing around generally and writing letters all about it to the folks at home. Orders came suddenly at lunch time to move to St. Fucien. Here in company with a few French soldiers the men spent the night in a mysterious old Château. St. Fucien is best remembered as the place where the guns were first clearly heard at their deadly work and their flashes seen.

Early the next morning the Battalion marched to Warfusée, a distance of about fourteen miles. The roads were in a shocking condition, and the going in full pack very heavy ; the men were very glad to reach billets.

The following week was spent here very comfortably

* The Battalion was not expected ; Mr. Williamson had gone forward with the transport.

among clean straw in Adrian huts. There was much routine yet to be got through in the way of fitting of box-respirators and other things. Nevertheless time was found for football, and bathing too, in spite of the month, in wagon-covers sunk in the ground.

During this week No. 9 Platoon under 2nd Lieutenant Chandler had their first taste of the line, being sent up in advance for a week's experience with a Gloucester Battalion. They rejoined safe and sound on the 10th very full of experiences and sights they very soon came to treat as items not worth mentioning. Major Rickman and No. 10 Platoon under Lieutenant Harrison were sent up on a like errand on the 14th, returning on the 17th, covered with mud if not with glory.

Meanwhile at noon on the 9th the Battalion had left Warfusée and moved to Foucaucourt. Warfusée at this time was just on the edge of the zone proper. In leaving it the Battalion left bricks and mortar, with connection between the two usually understood, and entered that desolate belt which stretches almost north and south from the sea to the Vosges Mountains, land across which those twin horsemen, Destruction and Death, had swept in all their fury, leaving only torn earth, shattered homesteads and pathetic little crosses to mark their passage.

It was here that the Battalion scroungers at last felt they could really let themselves go. The place, like most shelled and abandoned villages, was rich in discarded material of all sorts, and the huts and dug-outs were quickly made homely by additions calculated to add to comfort.

It was here, too, that an old iron tank found lying around was turned into a hot bath by the primitive but sufficient method of propping it on bricks and lighting a fire underneath. The only drawback to this system, as the too eager ones soon found, was that the bottom of the tank rapidly became red hot!

On the 17th the Germans in this sector commenced their now famous retirement, clearing the country as they went of everything likely to be of the slightest use to the

Allies. Trees and bushes were cut down, houses and huts burned, bridges destroyed, wells poisoned, and cross-roads blown in. Traps to catch the unwary were ingeniously sown in all directions and not the most innocent looking of bivvies or dug-outs could be trusted.

As a first result the Battalion found itself on fatigue duty making roads across the old No Man's Land in order that transport and heavy guns could move forward. Whilst on this work, the men saw what was to most of them their first dead German : almost a skeleton in rags of frayed and weather-soaked field-grey, he lay with extended arms on the Berny-Fresnes road. There he had rotted slowly between the lines through many weeks, caught probably on a raid or on one of those night expeditions into No Man's Land where men creep cautiously with their hearts in their mouths amid rank and tumbled vegetation. He would be posted as missing, and in some quiet village in Saxony his womenfolk would live hopefully on, dreaming against chance that he was a prisoner somewhere and would come back to them at the end of it all.

The next day the Battalion marched forward through Estrées to Brie. Here about 400 yards east of that place the 1st Battalion Northants was relieved in old German trenches named Bingen, Nassau, and Ulm,* whilst "D" Company, who had acted as advance guard, were in front on outpost duty at Mons-en-Chaussée.†

The next morning the consolidation of the Brie Bridgehead commenced. The Germans in their retirement across the Somme had, of course, blown all bridges, but the R.Es. had, in a remarkably short space of time, flung across a wooden structure capable of bearing most weights. Therefore, in order to protect this approach to our men on the east bank, properly fortified positions had to be constructed. As Sir Douglas Haig said in his despatch dealing with this period :

* Reference Map 62c S.W. 1/20,000. Bingen 0.29. Nassau 0.28. Ulm 0.27.

† Reference Map 62c S.E. 1/20,000 P.27.

The bridging of the Somme at Brie . . . is an example of the nature of the obstacles with which our troops were met and of the rapidity with which these obstacles were overcome. In this instance six gaps had to be bridged across the canal and river, some of them of a considerable width over a swift flowing stream. The work was commenced on the morning of 18th March, and was carried out night and day in three stages. By 10 p.m. on the same day foot-bridges for infantry had been completed. . . . Medium type bridges for horse transport and cavalry were completed by 5 a.m. on the 20th March, and by 2 p.m. on the 28th March . . . heavy bridges capable of taking all forms of traffic had taken the place of the lighter type.

The work mostly consisted in changing parados to parapet in the trenches already in existence and in dragging the wire entanglements from one side to the other. Quarters had been established in Athies Woods three-quarters of a mile away, but these had to be vacated and bivvies and shelters erected in and around the trenches worked upon.

Early on the 26th, orders arrived to move to Vraignes. Here the Battalion were billeted in evacuated houses with one company detached at Hancourt with outposts at Bernes and Fléchin and one platoon at Poeuilly. This day the Battalion had its first experience of close-hand shell-fire—three whizz-bangs landing near the column as it passed through Estrées-en-Chaussée.

A story is related of the neighbouring village of Bouvincourt which is worth mentioning here. The Germans had concentrated the local civil population in this village and, when retiring, left them there. The cavalry passing through a few days previously to ourselves found these poor refugees overwhelmed with joy to find themselves at last on the right side of the battle line. "Are you many?" queried one woman doubtfully to an officer. "We are two millions now," was the quiet reply.

The next day the Battalion moved on again, this time to Fléchin, where it relieved a company of Indian cavalry.

The Battalion was at last in the front line, but the experience was hardly that which it had been led to

expect. The men were billeted in ruined houses and
cellars. The outpost at Bernes rejoined, being relieved
by the 2/7th Battalion. Immediately on taking over,
defence work was begun, cruciform posts and trenches
dug and wired. It was during a daylight wiring party
that the Battalion suffered its first casualties : Corporal
Walker of " C " Company wounded, and Private Mace,
one of the pioneers, killed.

On the last day of March the 2/6th and 2/8th had
advanced against Vendelles and Soyecourt in splendid
order, but the story of that attack is told in another
volume. It is sufficient to say here that the Battalion
had witnessed this attack from the ruins of Fléchin, and
was now about to relieve the 2/7th, who had *gone over*
the previous night against the village of Le Verguier, but
without success. Tuesday morning, April 3rd, dawned
with promise of glorious sunshine, and the depression,
that overtakes the stoutest hearted during a night spent
in muddy wet quarters, was dispelled.

Suddenly the C.O. and Major Rickman were summoned
to Bernes to Brigade Headquarters. It was decided on
the spot that something was in the wind and that in
the near future there would be work of a more exciting
nature than that of digging and wiring the cruciform
posts which had been the occupation of the Battalion for
the last four days.

The officers were not kept long in suspense. A
message brought by Major Rickman, the acting Second-
in-Command, took the four officers commanding companies over to Vendelles, the village from which the
attack of the previous night had commenced. Here the
Colonel met them. On the way they gathered what
information they could from Major Rickman.

It appeared that the 2/7th had met with ill luck. The
difficulty of moving by night over ground which it had
been impossible to reconnoitre adequately beforehand,
had caused two attacking companies to lose direction and
the venture had failed. Le Verguier was still occupied
by the Germans and another attack must be made with

all speed. The 2/5th Battalion was to make this fresh attack and the C.O. and four company commanders now went to reconnoitre the ground from Vendelles.

Reconnaissance was difficult, as any approach nearer than 1,500 yards was certain of detection, and it was impossible to reach the ground over which the second attack was ultimately to take place. It was possible, however, to form a good idea of the position of the village, at any rate of its forward defences, which, in the light of after events, proved invaluable.

Situated on the highest point of a prominent ridge running north and south and parallel to the St. Quentin canal, the village of Le Verguier lies some 2½ miles to the north-east of Vendelles. The latter village rests upon a slightly lower spur of the same ridge which runs almost at right angles to the canal, the latter some six miles away to the east, with the main defences of the Hindenburg Line beyond. Between the two villages passed the Roisel-St. Quentin railway, crossing the Vendelles spur by a cutting to the north-west of Small Foot Wood. Typical of the modern results of early methods of village organization and agriculture, the ground between the two villages and the adjacent village of Jeancourt was covered with innumerable tracks, some of which might almost be termed roads, serving as communication for the villagers from their homesteads to their respective properties. Slightly below the crest-line of the Le Verguier ridge and protected by the natural feature of the railway, half a mile distance away, one of these tracks (that from Jeancourt to Maissemy) marked roughly the line of posts held by the 2/7th Battalion after their unsuccessful effort of the preceding night.

Nature had made Le Verguier seemingly impregnable. From the western edge of the village as far as eye could stretch one could see ridge after ridge of low undulating country rolling toward the Somme valley. Far to the north and south one had unequalled command from the ridge on which the village stood. It was ideal ground for a rearguard action with easy means of retirement if necessary : not a living being could approach unseen within 600 yards of the outer defences of the village. It was not to be wondered at that the German staff had decided to make this spot the battleground for the last stand their retiring troops were to make, before withdrawing to the believed impregnable Hindenburg Line, of which Ascension Ridge, a mile to the eastward, formed the outposts.

Reconnaissance took some four hours, and the company commanders returned to Fléchin in the late afternoon to find events had moved quickly in their absence. Almost everything was packed up and the companies were more or less ready to move. The night was to be spent in the reserve trenches in Vendelles, lately dug and occupied by the 2/7th on the north-east outskirts of the village. Only fighting personnel was taken and cookers were left behind at Fléchin for further orders.

The Battalion fell in at 7 o'clock in the evening in the order B.H.Q., "A," "B," "C" and "D" Companies, and moved at company intervals down the Vendelles road. It was then sunset, and it was estimated that the Battalion would arrive at Vendelles almost at dusk. With the exception of H.Q. officers and company commanders nobody knew exactly what was going to happen, but most surmised that they were at last going to take part in an attack. Until that day, with the exception of the favoured few, who had been in the line nearly a month before at Fresnes and Berny, not many had seen the enemy at closer quarters than 1,000 yards ; and all were eager to prove that the lengthy and tedious training of one of the last of the rapidly-formed divisions of the war had not been wasted.

Not many of those officers who took part in that march to Vendelles on the night of April 3rd will forget the sense of pride they felt in the men they commanded that day. Until that moment our casualties, including sick, could have been counted on both hands. As a fighting force the men were in the pink of condition, their training perfect and, with very few exceptions, only circumstances

over which they had no control prevented their being
seasoned veterans of the war.   There on the road could
be seen fellows who had enlisted in the Territorial Force
in the late summer of 1914, fully expecting to be part of
their glorious first line, yet whose fate led them to form
part of a second line Division detailed as a garrison for
the troubled Emerald Isle.   Again and again had they
commenced their dreary training : from Swanwick to
Dunstable ; from Dunstable to Watford, and finally to
the bleak plains of the Curragh an ironical destiny had
sent them when their first line comrades were entering
upon the Somme battles.   There, too, could be seen
Derby recruits of the best material, whose training had
been interrupted by a week's guerilla warfare and street-
fighting in the slums of Dublin.   A few there were also
who, caught by the belated Service Act, had endured the
first odium as conscripts and who, now that the moment
had come, were just as eager as their comrades to prove
their worth.   Last, but not least, were the first of the
young soldiers whose eighteenth birthday made them
part of the British fighting machine.   Curiously enough
nearly all the latter sprang from the West Riding of the
county of broad acres and had been destined to provide
the Battalion with its strongest sporting element for
many a day to come.

Such was the Battalion eager to prove its mettle.
Officers and men alike were imbued with one spirit—
to show that now they were at last on French soil they
could equal, if not surpass, their first line brethren, to
many of whom they were related by more than fellow
feelings.   Former troubles were forgotten : early and
seemingly wasted efforts at Swanwick ; the boiling hot
days of Dunstable Downs ; the long heavily-burdened
route-marches of Watford and the endless schemes of the
desolate Curragh entrenching area, all seemed nightmares
of an ugly past which was now to culminate in the longed
for opportunity.   As Nobby Chambers expressed it :
" What about company training now, boys! I'm
thinking them P.T. wallahs at Watford would come in

useful here!" Unconsciously he voiced the pent-up feelings of the Battalion which had been waiting two years for its chance.

Half a mile west of Vendelles the Battalion fell out to await guides who had been sent forward to reconnoitre our quarters for the night, and here they had a good opportunity of watching our divisional artillery in action, registering, as they afterwards knew, for the following day's barrage. Tremendously bucked by the bark of the 18-pounders the men were convinced the enemy must have been utterly miserable. It was then nearly dusk, and to check undue enthusiasm it began to rain slightly.

After nearly an hour's waiting the guides came back and led the Battalion to bivouacs for the night. As support Battalion the 2/5th were accommodated in the trenches north-east of Vendelles village, which had been occupied the previous night and day by the 2/7th Battalion who, when their attack had failed, had dug themselves in in new cruciform posts in front of the village, leaving their earlier trenches available for a supporting unit.

At 1.30 in the morning company commanders were summoned to Battalion Headquarters. Battalion Headquarters was in a cellar converted into a dug-out, and partly occupied by the 2/7th as well. Here they found the Commanding Officer, Major Rickman, and the Adjutant, surrounded by masses of the usual maps and papers; Lieutenants Smith and Williamson and the I.O., Lieutenant Kane, completed the conference. The last named had much information to give. During the previous day he had been absent on a reconnaissance which had taken him far behind Le Verguier, and which brought him back full of ideas.

The following is a copy of the *Operation Orders*, carried by runners through the rain in the early hours of that morning, April 4th, to the various company and headquarters' officers. It was read by the light from candles or torches in places sheltered from the wind. To all came the realization that now the real thing was upon them and the lessons learned in the mimic days were about to be put to the test.

OPERATION ORDERS
by
Lieut.-Col. G. H. St. Hill, T.D.

Commanding 2/5th Battalion, Notts and Derby Regiment.
Map, Ref. France Sheet 62 c N.E. &
62 c S.E.

1.   The Battalion will attack and capture at 7.0 a.m. to-morrow, 4th April, the village of *Le Verguier* and *Spur* 120 to the S.E.

It will then push on to *Grand Priel Woods* and establish touch with a battalion of the 177th Infantry Brigade about L.22 Central.

2.   The Battalion will parade in column of route in time to move off at 5.0 a.m., the head of the column resting on Battalion Headquarters, facing West in the following order : " A," " B," " D," and " C."

The Battalion will proceed in column of route to the railway at R.8 d 1.5 where it will halt.

Lieut A. J. KANE will lead the Battalion to this point. " A " Company will then wheel to the left and proceed in artillery formation in the direction indicated by Lieut. KANE, who will lead No. 1 Platoon.   " B " and " D " will conform.

The position prior to the attack will be south of the road running from R.3 Central to R.4 d 9.9.

Companies will be in lines extended to 5 paces and 50 yards distances.   " A " Company in front, followed by " B " and " D " Companies.   " C " Company will be in support 200 yards behind " D " Company and will remain in artillery formation.

3.   The artillery programme in support of the operation is as follows :

Wood and strong point in L.33.d. from 6 a.m. to 6.45 a.m. *Le Verguier* and *Spur* to the S.E. from 6 a.m. to 7 a.m. *Woods* L.28.d. from 7 a.m. to 7.15 a.m.   Then lift.

4.   At 6.40 a.m. the Left Platoon of " A " Company will advance and seize the wood and strong point in L.33.d.

At 6.55 a.m. the attack on the village and spur will be delivered.   Companies advancing in waves at 50 yards distance and extended to 5 paces.   " B " Company will drop a platoon to hold the spur.

When the village is captured " A " Company will push on to establish communication with 177th Brigade at *Grand*

Priel Woods and to construct a cruciform post at L.22.c.9.0.
(No. 1.)

" B " Company will dig a post at L.28.c.6.6. (No. 2) " D "
Company will dig a post at L.34.a.8.7. (No. 3) " C " will dig
a post at L.34.c.8.4. These posts should be carefully selected
to afford mutual support by Lewis-guns and to be slightly
retired from the forward slope of the crest of the hill. A
bombing party of 12 men, under Sergeant HUTCHINSON,
will be detailed by O.C. " C " Company to work up the
trench in conjunction with the remainder of the Battalion.

Lieut. G. H. WILLIAMSON will lead the party to the
entrance of the trench at the strong point R.2.b. " A "
Company will draw from Battalion Headquarters and carry
10 wire-cutters.

" C " Company will draw picks and shovels from Battalion
Headquarters, and on the capture of the village will deliver
picks and shovels to " A," " B," and " D " Companies, at
the No. 1, 2 and 3 cruciform posts ; one platoon will commence
digging No. 4 post.

R.E. material will be brought up by carrying parties of
the 2/6th Battalion.

During the consolidation, companies will send out patrols
and endeavour to keep in touch with the enemy.

Representative officers from each company will synchronize watches at Battalion Headquarters at 4.0 a.m. Each
Company will carry 10 ground flares ready to light in the
daytime for communication with aeroplanes.

They should be lit on any of our own aeroplanes sounding
a *Klaxon* horn.

One bombing section and one Lewis-gun will be on both
flanks of each company.

Regimental Aid Post will be at Battalion Headquarters
at *Vendelles*. Battalion Battle Headquarters will be at
strong point R.2.b. at 6.15 a.m., to which reports will be sent.

T. NADIN,

3/4/'17.   Captain and Adjutant.

The intention was to envelop the village from the
south. It was estimated that the German strength
was massed chiefly on the north-west side facing towards
Jeancourt, and that a frontal attack made by day would
fail for that reason. Observation had not located any
considerable defence on the south where trenches were
weak, and it was hoped that the remnants of the enemy
rearguard would be unable to protect their left flank

to the fullest extent if a portion of the attack was directed against their Jeancourt front. The attack was to consist of three waves, "A," "B," and "D" Companies respectively, with " C " Company in reserve to complete the consolidation of the positions won. The attacking troops were to assemble in the low ground west of the track crossing the Maissemy-Jeancourt ridge. In order to mask the main attack, and for the purpose of attracting the defence to the western front of the village, the left platoon of " A " Company (No. 4 Platoon under Lieutenant Adcock) was to make a frontal attack 10 minutes before zero and seize the enemy post, supposed to exist between Thierru Copse and the village itself, which was calculated, if not taken, to cause trouble by enfilade fire on the attacking waves.

Assuming the attack to be successful, it was intended that " A " Company should push forward through the village and occupy the high ground to the north-east in Grand Priel woods, whilst " C " Company and the rest of the Battalion consolidated the positions won immediately east of the village. Zero hour was fixed for 6.50 a.m., by which time it was anticipated there would be sufficient light to permit approach of an open character over ground which no one had been able to reconnoitre. (N.B. It must be borne in mind that the warfare was no longer of a trench nature, and that for the last three weeks the Germans had been retiring slowly on their Hindenburg defences). What artillery the Division now possessed was to concentrate, from zero until the attack reached the village, on the defences west of the village, after which the high ground in the rear was to be swept by shrapnel.

Optimistic as the troops were, there seemed no reason why, given suitable conditions, the plan should not succeed. Officers and men alike were more than enthusiastic and had fortune favoured their efforts the story of the attack would have been very different from actual events.

It was shortly after 3 a.m. when company commanders returned to their headquarters to explain the scheme to

their subalterns. Time was short. In order to reach
the place of assembly by the required hour it was necessary for the Battalion to leave its quarters by 5 a.m.
and before then there were a hundred-and-one things to
do. Breakfasts had to be served and eaten, blankets
collected, rations and the various impedimenta of attack,
which a thoughtful staff think essential to war, issued to
the unfortunate Tommies, and, above all, the scheme had
to permeate through to the men. To add to the discomfort it was now raining steadily, and the roads,
tracks and trenches, already churned up by the retiring
enemy, were slowly becoming a sea of mud and slime.

However, by 5.15 a.m. the Battalion had overcome its
early troubles and was able to move from Vendelles :
only just in time from the point of view of " A " and
" B " Companies whose quarters were vigorously shelled
by a 4.2 battery both as and after they left them. Time
worked out to perfection. A twenty minutes rest in
the railway-cutting allowed the companies to form up
10 minutes before zero. It was now fairly light, but although the rain had ceased to fall the sky was heavily
clouded.

For the first thirty minutes of the attack things went
well. No. 4 Platoon of " A " Company moved off to the
minute at 6.40 and disappeared from sight on their
mission of deluding the enemy from whose view, it was
anticipated, the remainder of the Battalion would be
concealed until within some 600 yards of the village,
when the nature of the ground would afford the opportunity of covered approaches from the south-east.

At 6.50 the attack began : "A " Company moved off,
followed at the requisite distance by " B " and " D "
Companies. Almost coincident with zero hour snow
began to fall, which proved a mixed blessing to the
Battalion at a later stage, although at the time the re-
marks of Captain Adams must have troubled the weather
prophet's conscience. In a few minutes the ridge was
breasted and the battle-ground in front and to the south
of the village was fully seen. Whether caught unawares

or not, strangely enough, the enemy took no notice of our approach until the high ground above the Caubrieres valley to the south of Le Verguier was reached, and it became necessary to descend the slopes of the Caubrieres Wood. Here the careful enemy had felled the trees, and as soon as the attacking waves reached the crest of the wood his distress signals soared to the sky. Even then the barrage put down by his guns, though of a heavy character, was badly directed and evidently only came from one battery. Far away on the left in front of the village the barrage was more effective, and apparently the attack of No. 4 Platoon was being regarded seriously (as had been hoped) by the Germans.

It was now snowing gently and the ground was rapidly becoming a sharp contrast to the dark outlines of the attacking figures ; and at that precise moment the enemy resorted to his machine-guns, cunningly concealed in the gardens stretching along the southern edge of the village. At first his fire was unheeded, as casualties were slight and the enemy seemed to have difficulty in getting the range, although it was then barely 800 yards. By this time too, the leading company had descended the incline of the Caubrieres Wood and was climbing the slope of the slight mound known as Odin Spur, crossed by the sunken track from Vendelles. This company was, moreover, well protected from the fire directed on the less fortunate supporting companies, but was more exposed to the shell-fire of the gunners. The sunken road was reached where a halt was made to allow the supporting companies to keep pace. Owing to the broken nature of the ground, this meant that companies gradually became intermingled.

In the sunken road matters now began to assume a serious aspect. Spotting the main attack was being directed on his weakest flank, the enemy opened a vigorous machine-gun fire on the crest of Odin Spur, behind which the leading company was waiting to press home the attack. At the same time a machine-gun post, at the junction of the sunken road and the German reserve line, realizing its advantageous position, was making the sunken road untenable to the attacking troops. This post, however, was effectively silenced by Sergeant Orgill's platoon, whose Lewis-guns were ably directed by their leader on to it ; it now became possible for the attacking waves to rush down the hill without fear of dangerous enfilade from the right and exposed flank.

Time could not be wasted; 200 yards down the slope of Odin Spur was dead ground from which it was thought the attack could easily be pushed home into the gardens and streets of the village. In any case it was under good cover where reorganization would be possible.

Down the hill raced No. 2 Platoon led by Sergeant Orgill, followed immediately by No. 1 Platoon under Lieutenant Rossiter on the extreme right, with No. 3 Platoon on the left under Lieutenant Wright ; close behind followed the supporting companies, and none too soon. It was the only way out of the difficult situation in which the Battalion found itself, and even then the machine-guns took heavy toll as the companies swept down the ridge, now white with a coating of snow, against which the khaki masses were sharply outlined. Away to the left above Thierru Copse, two machines-guns, in the ground believed to be taken by No. 4 Platoon, played havoc with their fire, catching the troops as they rushed down the spur to the haven of the hollow below. Too, vigorous enfilade and frontal fire was making the descent of the gentle slope of Odin Spur a path of lead through which it seemed a miracle for anything to move alive.

Once in the hollow, it was obvious to all that the attack had miscarried. Out of some 450 attacking troops only 150 men were effective in the valley below the village and these were now separated from the reserve company by nearly ¾ mile of difficult and bullet-swept ground. Touch moreover had, owing to the snow, been lost with No. 4 Platoon on the left, and it was impossible to tell whether Lieutenant Adcock had found Thierru post occupied or not. In any case his platoon must have

F

been held up, or its assistance could not have failed to counteract the merciless fire from the ground above Thierru Copse. Four runners, three of whom never returned, had unsuccessfully endeavoured to find this luckless platoon. Six officers still remained, and Captain Stebbing and Captain Trench decided that until support could be given on the left it was hopeless to cross the 300 yards of slope which separated the hollow from the village. The Battalion was in fact in a pocket from which there was no escape, but provided covering support could have been given on its left, it could easily have emerged and forced a foothold in the village. An "appreciation of the situation" was hurriedly sent back to Battalion Headquarters in Small Foot Wood ; companies were reorganized as far as posible and an effort was made to consolidate the position in which they found themselves.

Only now did they realize the cost of the attack. Looking back towards the slopes of Caubrieres Wood and Odin Spur, from the hollow in which they were placed, they could see dozens of inert forms being gradually covered by the falling snow. Away back behind the sunken road Captain Adams had fallen, his right leg blown to atoms by the near burst of a 5.9. At the bottom of Odin Spur lay Lieutenant Rossiter, still the target for sniping-fire. The hill slopes told a vivid story of the attack and the accuracy of the German gunners. It was not to be wondered that the few surviving in Thierru hollow imagined fate was against them.

Fresh to the mind two incidents of the hollow still recall the self-sacrifice shown by the average British Tommy when the safety of others is at stake.

Lieutenant Rossiter lay where he had fallen some 100 yards short of the immunity of the hollow. He had been badly wounded by a bullet through the lung. To reach him seemed certain death, but unless he was protected from the snow, his chances of recovery were small. Moreover, the enemy from his posts in front of the village was amusing himself by sniping from 300 yards range at any wounded where movement showed any sign of life. As soon as he realized his officer's predicament, Private Brown, Lieutenant Rossiter's runner, a Yorkshire lad aged 19, went out to his commander, covered him up with his own waterproof sheet and remained by his side until it became possible to carry him to a place of safety. Three times afterwards snipers succeeded in hitting Lieutenant Rossiter, but, strange to say, Brown remained untouched.

One more example of a runner's devotion to duty was given by Private Graham, the simple heroic nature of whose action only those who witnessed it can realize the value. If the attack was to be brought to a successful conclusion, or for that matter, if the remnants of the Battalion were to be secured, support must be obtained from either flanking units in the line or the Battalion reserve in the rear. To cross alive the slopes of Odin Spur and Caubrieres Wood seemed impossible. Four runners had failed to get touch with No. 4 Platoon, and, through their efforts to cross the ground commanded by the village, were known to be dead. Yet by some means a message must reach Battalion Headquarters quickly, if support was to be forthcoming before the enemy howitzers located our position. Volunteers were asked for; at least a dozen stood forward, of whom Private Graham was the first. He not only took the message, but returned within the hour. The action well illustrates the spirit animating this sturdy " half-back " collier from the north. It was this selfsame spirit which lay behind the ultimate success of the British two years later. Actions like these will be remembered and will, let it be hoped, help much to clinch the bonds of sympathy between all ranks and will hold fast long after the war. No length of time or difference of station will ever eradicate that sense of fellowship between those who have looked together into the face of death whether in the successful attacks of 1917, or during the German wave of victory in the following March.

Nine o'clock came and passed; matters were getting

more desperate. So far the German had not succeeded in gauging our whereabouts with his high-angle fire, although a few isolated shells showed he was not ignorant of the existence of Thierru hollow. Sooner oɪ later he was bound to reach it. His observers in the village must have been fully aware of the presence of our survivors within 250 yards of their stronghold. He could not let us remain there until dark without danger to himself. Occasional bursts of machine-gun fire from the village gardens raked the top of the hollow, covered the slope of Odin Spur and gave our men to understand that no further approach would be allowed to the village by day, and certainly no withdrawal, although until that moment no one had thought of anything but getting into the village at all costs. Once inside a village one hundred and fifty men can cause infinite trouble to its occupiers. It now became a question whether sufficient support could be obtained, from flank and rear, to occupy the attention of the enemy machine-guns hindeɪing the crossing of the slope intervening between the hollow and the garden south of the village.

The attackers had not long to wait for an answer. To everybody's surprise, Colonel St. Hill, in his usual old white mackintosh, and accompanied by Sergeant-Major Cope, were seen coming down the slope of Odin Spur. Why they were not hit was a puzzle. Until that moment nothing had remained alive on that portion of the hill. Luckily the snow had turned to a blinding storm which may have hidden them, as it later concealed the retreating remnants, from the attentions of the German snipers. All were more than pleased to see them, expecting that now the reserve company would be able to assist the attack.

When the situation was reported to Colonel St. Hill, he said, " How the hell did you fellows get down here alive ? " Very quickly he summed up the circumstances. Sufficient support could not be forthcoming in time to be of use for a further attack that day, the numbers remaining were hopelessly inadequate to attack the village held by a force thrice that estimated. The Battalion must with-draw somehow or other before the few that were left were shelled out of the cover in which they were endea-vouring to dig themselves in. Further attack was definitely hopeless. Whether Fate wished to make amends for the disastrous failure one cannot say. Had it not been for the snow, which now settled down to a steady blinding storm, impenetrable by the eye for more than 100 yards, no withdrawal could possibly have been effected without leaving most of the remainder as corpses on Odin Spur. As luck had it the snow, which had made us easy targets for German riflemen, now, aided by a driv-ing south-east wind, turned to a regular blizzard through which no machine-gunner could direct his sights. Slowly the shattered remnants of "A," "B," and "D" Companies withdrew by sections to the high ground above Caubrieres Wood, whilst "C" Company covered their withdrawal from the sunken road across Odin Spur and from the forward slope of Caubrieres Wood, though protection in the withdrawal seemed needless. The blizzard effected what rifle-fire could barely have done, and the Battalion was able to haul back to safety most of the dead and wounded who covered the slopes. Untiring work was done by "C" Company and the regimental stretcher-bearers who, long after the withdrawal was complete, were occupied in taking back the dead and wounded, until the lifting of the storm rendered it impos-sible to recover more bodies. When one remembers the heaviness of the ground through snow and mud, and that every case had to be carried nearly two miles to the nearest Aid Post, one will realize what sterling work those fellows did, many of them making four and five journeys to the slopes of the Battalion's first battlefield. Lastly one still sees the return of the party bringing back Lieutenant Rossiter, with Private Brown begging to be allowed to remain with him until he knew that he was safe.

Meanwhile what had happened to No. 4 Platoon? Reaching Vendelles it was found that none had returned,

although one man was known to have passed through a
dressing-station behind the Battalion's right front. This
was possible, as the ground was fresh to all ranks and men
could easily lose their way. Enquiry, however, proved
that Lieutenant Adcock, the platoon officer, had been
wounded early in the action, and had been despatched
to a dressing-station in the Vermand direction by the
stretcher-bearers of another unit. The attack was
therefore carried on by Sergeant Stone, of whom a glowing
account was given by the survivors twelve hours later,
when Lance-Corporal Dwyer and seven men were all that
darkness allowed to withdraw of the forty that originally
set out.

It appeared that Lieutenant Adcock was wounded
shortly after the platoon disappeared from the view of
the rest of the company, and that Sergeant Stone on
taking charge mistook the position, against which the
attack was to be directed, to be the ground on the western
outskirts of the village. This was more than possible as,
once snow had fallen, no landmarks could be picked out
to serve as guidance. Actually the platoon crossed
unoccupied the ground on which it should have remained,
and from there, owing to the snow, direction was even
further lost, resulting in the platoon directly crossing
the enemy front in the teeth of a murderous fire at 400
yards' range. The platoon now found itself on the
westward slope of the Le Verguier-Vendelles ridge, and
hidden from view from the rest of the Battalion, and
there it certainly achieved the object of attracting the
enemy's attention to his Jeancourt front.

It seemed that from his own position Sergeant Stone
could follow the attack of the remaining companies for
some time, and he conjectured that by occupying the
western edge of the village with his platoon, the enve-
loping attack of the rest of the Battalion to the south
would be assisted.

His platoon followed him to a man, recognizing the
superbness of their leader's dogged bravery. Two
trenches at right-angles to the position, and three belts

of wire, had to be negotiated before the platoon found itself in free ground to manœuvre, and, by then, its numbers were sadly depleted. Wounded himself in crossing the first belt of wire, Sergeant Stone still led his men on until a second bullet brought him down beyond the last belt; even then he continued bravely directing his platoon until killed by a sniper. Only about fifteen men remained and several of these were badly wounded. To reach the village was impossible. A few shell-holes behind a low hedge 200 yards from the village were all the cover available, and there until dark the fifteen men remained under the charge of Lance-Corporal Dwyer, only surviving N.C.O. Withdrawal for them was impossible and for twelve hours they remained in the shell-holes before the village, keeping up intermittent fire upon the foe, trying to prevent his fire becoming effective on the wounded who lay in the open. Communication between shell-holes was fatal, and seven of the fifteen lost their lives in endeavouring to reach wounded comrades on the ground beside them.

Such was the story gathered from the survivors. Afterwards, when the village was taken by the Battalion a week later, their story proved correct, as the blackened corpses of Sergeant Stone and his men bore witness.

Sergeant Stone was a brave man and one of the N.C.Os. of whom the Battalion has reason to be proud. Idol of his platoon, brilliant half-back of his company football team, popular alike with officers and men, he died as he had lived, doing his best. No one who knew him could fail to like the quiet way in which he controlled men, and the cheerful discipline by which he succeeded in getting things done. Reliable and trustworthy to the last, even in death, he infected his men with that quiet spirit of bravery which marked his character. His whole company loved him, and when, a week later, his body was laid to rest in the little cemetery at Vendelles, sacred to the memory of many of the Battalion, one Tommy expressed his honest feeling for the young N.C.O. in these

words, " 'E was a lad, our Sergeant," and in this epitaph
the Battalion concurred.

> For to do more than you can
> Is to be a British man—
> Not a rotten " also ran ".
>   " Carry on."

Last in No. 4 Platoon to be killed was Private Pidcock.
His was simply another instance of the real worth which
lies beneath the surface of the Derby man.   Pidcock was
the only son of a widowed mother.   He had heard his
country's call and enlisted in 1915.   After his recruit's
training was over, he became officers' mess waiter and
ultimately, on reaching France, a company mess cook.
On the morning of the attack on Le Verguier he was
detailed to remain in Vendelles, but he begged hard to be
allowed to accompany his platoon.   " It's the first real
show, sir !   Let me go."   It was a request that could not
be resisted and Pidcock joined the thousands of his sort
who gave their lives for their country.   He was a straightforward Tommy out to help as best he could, whether
his work lay in the looking after the welfare of others
or in giving his all in a Great Adventure to make the
world better by his gift.   He was killed, shot through the
head, whilst endeavouring to reach Sergeant Stone.

The attack was over.   It had failed and failed badly.
Nothing could now be done except dig in closer to the
enemy, and for that purpose " C " Company, who had
already worked hard carrying back wounded and covering
the Battalion's withdrawal, was detailed to dig cruciform
posts in front of the original positions of assembly.
Indeed " C " Company was alone available for this task,
as the remaining companies were far too weak to be of
any real use for rapid work, which was then imperative.
" A " Company, on whom the brunt of the attack had
fallen, had suffered over eighty casualties and other companies had fared little better.   It was a sorry story.

Looked at in the light of later stages of open warfare
at the close of hostilities, the tactics of attack used in
after months might have succeeded.   But those tactics,

we must remember, were the evolution of the fighting of the summer of 1917. In the spring of that year, our army was still harnessed to a method of trench-warfare useless in the open. But, even given altered tactics and formations, much allowance must be made for an enemy strength thrice that estimated, for artillery inadequate for the magnitude of the task, and for an ignorance of the ground which, in the time allowed for the attack, it was impossible to remedy. The men were there, but fate decreed that, through circumstances over which they had no control, their first efforts should be doomed to failure.

Relieved by the 2/7th in the early evening, the Battalion moved back, taking its dead and wounded with it. Tired out, the men slept the night away in the comparative luxury and safety of cellars in Vendelles. The casualties were : killed 1 officer (Captain Adams), 19 other ranks ; wounded 4 officers, 80 other ranks.

The weather cleared and the next morning was bright and springlike. The men were refreshed after a good night's rest. The Brigadier sent a letter which was read to all ranks, and ran, " Will you convey to the 2/5th Battalion my deep appreciation of their brave attempt to capture Le Verguier this morning. They behaved as I knew they would, and I deplore the heavy losses incurred."

Very little besides resting was done in the morning, but in the afternoon, on the south-eastern corner of Vendelles and close to the French cemetery, the Battalion buried the dead who had fallen in the previous morning's attack.

The next day was Good Friday, and that evening the Battalion stood-to as reserve to the 2/6th and 2/8th who were to make one more attempt on Le Verguier. It was a night of high wind and snow. With daylight came the depressing news that this attack too had failed. As dusk fell the Battalion moved up and relieved the 2/7th in the cruciform posts before Le Verguier.

Saturday and Sunday passed quietly enough. The sun appeared and our fellows dried themselves out and

recovered their usual spirits.   At dusk on Easter Sunday
" A " Company were detailed to dig jumping-off trenches
for an attack in force the following day.

But at 6 a.m. on the 9th the Division on our right
reported that the enemy had evacuated the trenches in
R.5. and R.12 ; the 184th Brigade pushed forward
patrols and occupied these trenches.   The 2/5th sent out
patrols composed of battalion snipers and bombers, and
by 9 a.m. these had penetrated Le Verguier and found
it evacuated.   Two companies, advancing in support
(the men carrying their Easter parcels (!) which had just
arrived), went right through the village and commenced
to dig themselves in on the north side, whilst two companies moved to German trenches in L.34, R.4 and R.5.
No. 12 Platoon under Mr. Chandler were just in time to
see the enemy rearguard running for dear life from the
northern outskirts of the village.   Legend relates that
our men gave chase, but in this case the devil had wings
in the shape of fear, and got safely away.

The line was consolidated by the digging of rifle-pits
from L.28.a.9.5. through the copse at L.28.d.o.o. to L.34.
b.2.0, L.34.d.6.0. and on to approximately R.5.a.6.4. *
The whole operation was carried through without much
opposition, the casualties being eight other ranks killed,
and one officer and eleven other ranks wounded.   The
consolidation of positions was continued throughout
the night and following day.   Snow fell again and the
men were glad to work to keep themselves warm and to
improve their somewhat cramped quarters in the hastily
dug pits.   An attempt by Lieutenant P. P. Harrison to
occupy Ascension Farm, which was reported evacuated
at midday on the 10th, proved unsuccessful.

Our line was heavily shelled by the enemy.   Private
Harrison, No. 1 in a Lewis-gun post, had a narrow escape
from a whizz-bang which exploded near enough to him
to blow his gun several yards away.   C.S.M. Tomlinson,
realizing that the shell must have fallen uncommonly
close, strolled along to see what damage had been done.

* Map sheets 62 c N.E. and 62 c S.E. 1/20,000.

" Are you all right, Harrison ? " " Oh yes, sir, but will you pass me my gun ? "

That night the Battalion was heartily glad to be relieved by the 2/5th South Staffords, and moved back through Jeancourt to Brigade reserve in Bernes, where it spent the next eight days in providing working parties for the roads, which, owing to the heavy rain and still heavier traffic over them, were badly in need of repair.

Just previously there had been big changes in the 59th Divisional staff, and on the 13th the 2/5th had an opportunity of seeing its new Brigadier, General Stansfeld, when he came to inspect it. Four days later the new Divisional Commander, General Romer, watched the Battalion carry out a practice attack.

As a sequel to its share in the occupation of Le Verguier the following message received from F.M. Sir Douglas Haig was published in Battalion Orders. " I congratulate you on the successful results of yesterday's operations. Convey to the troops and formations that took part in them, my appreciation of the gallantry and skill shown by them."

On the 18th, the Battalion moved up again into the Grand Priel sector, taking over Brigade support from the 2/5th Battalion Leicesters at Hervilly ; " A " Company going on half a mile to the next village Hesbecourt. Three very comfortable days were spent here in cellars, stables and one long hut, which accommodated most of the men. The hut the Germans had apparently intended to destroy, but had left it till too late. Evidences of his occupation of the village were everywhere—in the deliberately levelled fruit trees and in the graves with elaborate headstones over his dead in the cemetery. These latter were in excellent order and undisturbed, but the heavy flat stone slabs covering the family vaults of the villagers had been shifted, and peering downwards one could see in some of them a disorder of clothing, ripped portmanteaux and cases strewn about. Remnants, probably, of valuables deposited there by refugees in their attempts to find a safe hiding-place.

The strength of the Battalion at this time had been reduced to 16 officers and 467 other ranks. This was partly compensated for by the arrival during April of 7 more officers, 4 of whom came from The Buffs.

On the night of the 22nd the "rest" came to an end with the relief of the 2/8th Battalion Sherwood Foresters in the line just south of Villeret. "C" and "D" Companies were located in a series of advanced posts on a line running approximately north and south from L. 17. b. 9.4. to Château L.23. c.8.5. "B" Company were in support on the main line of resistance nearly a mile behind on a properly dug and wired trench-system lying in rear of Grand Priel Wood, L.22. a. 3.4. to L.16. a. 7.5., and "A" Company were in reserve in Carpeza Copse at L.15.* The 2/7th held the remainder of the Brigade frontage on our left. They were afterwards relieved on the 28th by "B" Company 2/5th Battalion.† This tour of duty, which lasted until the beginning of May, was on the whole quiet. The enemy had reached the end of his voluntary retirement and was heavily entrenched behind previously prepared defences, with many yards of barbed-wire, on the crest of the further ridge. Between our advanced posts and his main line the ground swept gracefully down into a broad valley to rise again fairly steeply to his positions holding the Canal. Practically every tree in Grand Priel had been levelled, but spring spoke in the air and in the wild flowers that peeped from amid the litter of trunks and branches of felled trees.

But for exceptional strafes, the men had little to do except write home or lie on their backs in the sun and watch the aeroplanes for ever busy overhead.

On the night of the 27th the outpost line was definitely advanced about 500 yards from the roadway south of Villeret to a further series of posts on the crest of the rise, thus giving us command of the valley below. This was accomplished without opposition, but the new posts and

* Reference Map sheets 62. c. N.E. 62. c. S.E. 1/20,000.
† Reference Map 62. c. N.E. and S.E. 1/20,000. Main Line of
    Resistance ran from L.4. b. o.6. to L.16. a. 8.8.

the wire erected before them attracted notice the next day and received some violent shelling. The wire thus blown down was re-erected as soon as darkness fell.

One early morning at 3 a.m., whilst going round re-calling the "screen" to the wiring party, Sergeant Turner saw what he thought to be the end man lying unresponsive and apparently asleep. Going up he shook the figure and discovered it to be a dead German.

The following night Sergeant Offiler and his men dug a grave and, repeating what they knew of the Burial Service, buried the man, and placed there a rough wooden cross to mark the spot bearing the words, "Body of unknown German Soldier P. Straam." From letters and identifications it was discovered that the man was a German warrant-officer named Straam, but in spite of this, our boys could not resist the use of that phrase, so common a sight and yet withal so pathetic and simple, "body of an unknown soldier."

The casualties during the period were two other ranks killed, and one officer wounded.

In the dark hours of May 1st-2nd, the 2/6th Battalion Sherwoods came and took over the line, the 2/5th returning, one company to Hesbecourt and the remainder to their old billets in Hervilly.

The same morning it was officially announced that the Battalion would take part in an attack on Cologne and Malakoff Farms. It was not unprepared for this announcement. These two farms were situated a mile east of Hargicourt and about a quarter of a mile apart on high ground, and formed strong and well fortified outposts to the German main Siegfried system.

Several attacks by other units in the Divisions had been made on these points. On April 27th, the 2/6th and 2/8th Battalions Sherwood Foresters had attacked and captured the famous Hargicourt Quarries, but, so far, Cologne and Malakoff had successfully resisted all assaults.

Therefore, early on the 2nd, company commanders rode off into Roisel for a council of war at Brigade Head-

quarters, where the G.O.C. Division outlined the general
plan of attack and the artillery programme was decided
upon. The operation was to take place on the night of
May 3rd, and there was no time to be lost.

That afternoon, therefore, Os.C. companies went up
into the front line to make their final reconnaissance of
the Farms, and the surrounding ground. Upon their
return everything was finally settled, and orders were
accordingly published on the morning of the 3rd as
follows :

No. 2.
May 2nd, 1917.

OPERATION ORDERS
by

Major R. B. Rickman, Commanding
2/5th Battalion, Notts and Derby Regiment.

Ref.:—Maps, Sheet 62. c. N.E. and Special Divisional Map No. 63.

1.   INTENTION.—On the night 3-4th May the Battalion will
attack *Malakoff* and *Cologne Farms*.
2.   OBJECTIVES.—For the attack on *Malakoff Farm* there will
be two objectives.
(i) The trench running W. of the Farm from L.6. a. 28.55. to
F.30. c. 38.25. connecting up on the right with a bombing
block which will be established on the night 2-3rd May, by
the 2/8th Sherwood Foresters, at L.6. a. 35.48.
A block will be formed on the left of this objective.
(ii) The road running on the N.E. side of *Malakoff Farm*
from about F.30. c. 9.1. to about F.30. c. 70.45.
When this objective is taken it will be held by two posts of
one complete platoon each. The remainder of the attacking
force will then be withdrawn to the first objective.
The forming-up place will be the switch trench in L.5. b. and
F.29. d.
For the attack on *Cologne Farm* there will be two objectives.
(i) The first objective will be the trench S.W. of *Cologne
Farm* from L.6. c. 5.2. to L.6. c. 2.6. Blocks will be formed
on the right and left.
(ii) The second objective will be the trenches immediately E.
of *Cologne Farm* at L.6. c. 6.4. and L.6. c. 5.7. Blocks will be
formed on both flanks. The block on the right will be at the
junction of the two trenches at L.6. c. 84.26. The forming-
up place will be rear of the trench on eastern lip of the Quarry
at L.6. c. 9.3. After the capture of the 2nd objective O.C.

Right-half Battalion (see para. 3) will send a strong patrol
to see if the Factory in G.1. b. can be seized and held.

3. DISPOSITION.—" B " and " D " Companies (Left-half
Battalion) will carry out the attack on *Malakoff Farm*, and
will be under the command of Captain R. C. TRENCH.
" A " and " C " Companies (Right-half Battalion) will
carry out the attack on *Cologne Farm*, and will be under the
command of Captain T. H. L. STEBBING.

4. THE ATTACK.—The attack will be carried out in two waves
of two lines each as arranged by the commanders of the
Right and Left-half Battalion respectively. Bombers and
rifle-grenadiers will be on the flanks in order that the blocks
mentioned in para. 2 may be formed immediately the objectives are captured.

5. BARRAGE.—Artillery and machine-gun barrages are being
arranged and details will be issued later.

6. ROUTE TO POSITION OF DEPLOYMENT.—*Hervilly-Hesbecourt*
(where " A " Company will join the Battalion)—to L.10. a.
4.5. (Battle Headquarters) where Lieut. G. H. Williamson
and his guides will lead Right-half Battalion to position of
deployment.
Left-half Battalion will proceed to its position under its own
guides.

7. BATTALION BATTLE HEADQUARTERS ⎫
8. REGIMENTAL AID POST   ⎬ Will be at L.10. a. 4.5.
9. BATTALION DUMP   ⎭

10. ADVANCED BRIGADE HEADQUARTERS Will be at *Ruelles
Wood* at L.7. d. 7.7.

11. DRESS.—Fighting order as laid down by Division. In
addition each man will carry one pick or one shovel and an
extra sandbag. Rifle-grenadiers 12 grenades each.

12. Watches will be synchronized at Battalion Headquarters
Hervilly at 6. p.m., May 3rd. Zero will be at 11.30 p.m.,
May 3rd.

13. The head of the Battalion will pass N.E. exit from *Hervilly*
at 8 p.m. Order of march :—" C," " B," " D," 50 paces
between platoons. Lewis-gun wagons will be behind the leading platoon of each company. The wagons will be unloaded
as quickly as possible on arrival at Battle Headquarters.

14. One signalling N.C.O. and two signallers only per company
will take part in the attack, unless extra men are specially
detailed by the Signalling Officer.

15. Packs and stores will be stacked in the present quarters under
company arrangements, and left in charge of sick men under
the R.S.M.

16. The rum ration will be issued as late as possible.

17. Attention is drawn to the following points which should be
brought to the notice of all ranks :—

(*a*) After passing through gaps in barbed-wire, parties must at once spread out and reform their line.

(*b*) All deployments and movements must be performed with the greatest care and in dead silence.

(*c*) The importance of immediate consolidation. Under no circumstances is souvenir hunting to be allowed.

(*d*) Men should get as close as possible to the supporting barrage and kneel down.

(*e*) Bunching is to be avoided.

(*f*) The iron ration and Friday's ration will be carried on the men. Economy in water must be impressed, as a bottle may have to last 48 hours.

(*g*) All parties in captured trenches must at once protect their flanks.

(*h*) Positions captured must be held at all costs, as counter-attacks are to be expected.

(*i*) Every effort must be made to send back information.

T. NADIN,
Captain and Adjutant,
2/5th Battalion,
Notts and Derby Regiment.

ADDENDUM NO. 1 to 2/5th OPERATION ORDER No. 2.

1. In continuation of para. 5 of Operation Order No. 2 the attack will be made under cover of artillery barrages as shown on a copy of Special Divisional Map No. 63.
This is the only copy issued to the Battalion, and maps No. 63 in possession of officers can be marked up from this map at Battalion Headquarters, *Hervilly.*
It is improbable that any further copies of Map No. 63 can be obtained, copies of such parts of this map—as affects companies—must be taken from maps issued.

2. The 175th Machine-gun Company will fire upon—
The copse in F.30. c. 9.8.
The Sugar Factory.
Copse in G.2. a.
The cutting in L.12. a.
Will establish barrages through F.30. a. and A.25. Central, and through G.7. a. and G.7. c.

3. A contact aeroplane can be expected at 6 a.m. on 4th May.

T. NADIN,
Captain and Adjutant,
2/5th Battalion, Notts and Derby Regiment.

May the 3rd was spent in explaining the scheme to the men and in practising the method of the attack, until everybody understood at least his part in the forthcoming operations.

RUINED VILLAGE—THE SALIENT.

[See page 104

THE ENCLO-SURE.

FOKKER FARM.

KANSAS CROSS.

KANSAS CROSS—ZONNEBEEKE ROAD (after heavy shelling).

[See *page* 105

By 7 p.m. all was in readiness, and the Battalion marched out of Hervilly and Hesbecourt to their places of assembly. "A" and "C" Companies to the Quarries and "B" and "D" to the front line before Malakoff, then being garrisoned by the 2/8th Battalion. Here a trench known as Enfilade Trench ran from our front line to that of the enemy. It was held at our end by a bombing block supported by one Stokes-gun. According to plan the 2/8th should have bombed down this trench as a preliminary to our attack, but owing to a misunderstanding this was apparently not done.

At 11.30 p.m. our barrage came down and the advance began. "B" and "D" Companies' objectives were (1) a trench 600 yards long and situated 100 yards in front of Malakoff, and 400 yards away from our jumping-off point in Switch Trench, and (2) the road on the far side of the Farm itself.

Now in front of the first objective, and near its extremities, two gaps had been cut by the artillery in the wire, and it had been decided to push the attack through the one on the right. A wire was laid by Lieutenant Alliban from our line to the gap which would act as a guide to the four platoons of "B" Company as they followed each other through it. The first platoon under 2nd Lieutenant Jordan was to carry on across the trench and rush some rifle-pits near the Farm. The other three platoons were to rush the trench itself and clear it, to the left as far as a small strong-point (which was the left boundary), and on the right as far as a thick belt of wire adjacent to Enfilade Trench (the right boundary of attack).

Following "B" Company were three platoons of "D" Company whose job it was to go straight ahead, pass the Farm on the right, and dig themselves two posts in suitable positions on the east side of the Farm. The fourth platoon of "D" Company under 2nd Lieutenant Waters was to be held in reserve.

The attack succeeded fairly well, though owing to the very few men who got through the gap in the first few minutes the clearing of the first objective to the left was

G

not carried out in sufficient force. This work, in fact, for a time devolved almost entirely upon Lieutenant Groner and Sergeant Charlton who performed wonders. The German garrison quickly realized the weakness of the attackers, counter-attacked, and, in spite of the heroic efforts of Lieutenant Groner and his little band to stem the rush, managed to reoccupy about 250 yards of the trench, leaving us with about the same length defended by a bombing block and a Lewis-gun. On the other hand 2nd Lieutenant Jordan's platoon were completely successful, and their objective, the rifle-pits, taken.

The three platoons of " D " Company were somewhat slow in finding their way to their destination and for a long time Lieutenants Alliban and Lavender had only a dozen men to help them dig their posts. Eventually all stragglers arrived.

The remainder of the night was spent in consolidation, but, as frequently happens even in the most carefully planned attack, picks and shovels failed to arrive and the next day was spent by the men lying full length in shallow limestone trenches or shell-holes, beneath a blazing sun.

With daylight came the realization that the positions held were extremely precarious.

Enfilade Trench was still occupied by the enemy as was also both flanks of First Objective Trench. In addition, it became clear, from the continual sniping from the rear, that the sunken road in the old No Man's Land which had been taken by "B" and "D" in their first stride contained dug-outs still in possession of the Germans. Furthermore, between First Objective Trench and the front posts lay felled trees, in what once had been the orchard of Malakoff Farm, and amongst these lay numerous Germans who had been put to flight in the first flush of our attack.

The position really was untenable, and the line should have been withdrawn at the earliest opportunity without waiting for the counter-attack which was bound to come.

During the afternoon an enemy aeroplane circled low

over the captured ground, undoubtedly taking in both our numbers and positions. Later the posts were shelled and gas shells dropped in the valley behind us to hamper any reinforcements that might be contemplated. At 7.30 p.m. a message was received at Headquarters that the enemy could be seen by our forward posts massing for an attack in wood A.26. Central, and artillery was directed to this spot.

At dusk came the expected. Our S.O.S. went up from Malakoff and Lieutenant Alliban sent back word that his posts were being attacked by a force consisting of four or five waves each about one hundred strong. Instead of making straight for our front posts the attackers swerved to the right with the intention of cutting them off. Lieutenant Jordan's platoon was sent up to reinforce, but were unable to stop the rush. In order to avoid losing all his men Lieutenant Alliban ordered a retirement to the trench in rear. He himself was the last to attempt to withdraw, but too late. By this time the enemy were upon him, and he went down fighting with his fists. This was the last ever seen or heard of a very gallant and courageous officer.

In the confusion the men withdrawing from the forward posts went over First Objective Trench instead of making a stand with the "B" Company garrison there. The men of "B" Company, imagining that a general retirement had been ordered, followed them. In consequence both flanks gave and the Germans continuing their circling movement, the whole line fell back to the sunken road. Here a stand was made, but eventually, owing to the impossibility of consolidating and holding this road, Captain Trench ordered the withdrawal to Switch Trench.

Meanwhile on the right how had things gone with "A" and "C" Companies in their assault on Cologne ? Here the opposing lines were only a short distance apart. So near were they in fact that, economically, friend and foe utilized the same belt of barbed-wire defences.

In this the artillery had cut a gap which had been kept open by machine-gun fire. The plan was to rush this gap and bomb to the flanks whilst the platoons following were to carry on, take Cologne Farm, and consolidate on the further side of it. A platoon from " A " Company under Lieutenant Harrison was to complete the operation by going through to Unnamed Farm (midway between Malakoff and Cologne), which it was judged to be held in no great force, and thus link up the four companies in their new positions.

When " A " and " C " Companies lined up they were told that instead of a single gap there were two, and the original plan had to be changed during the last few minutes before zero.

Almost immediately our guns started the enemy barrage came down with great intensity. Even the machinegun nests around Malakoff directed their fire upon "A" and "C" Companies, not at first realizing that they too had a show to themselves.

So effective was the counter-barrage that many were caught before they left the jumping-off trench, and only three, Lieutenant Whiston, Sergeant Crowe and Private Mart, got through the wire. As the men advanced across the open, machine-guns caught them in enfilade and their withering fire did great damage. The enemy barrage on the Quarry, too, was very heavy, causing casualties in the reserve platoons. At 12.40 a.m. the survivors of the attacking party withdrew under cover of machine-gun fire from the 2/8th Sherwood Foresters' post at L.5. d. 9.4. and support from 178th Brigade Trench Mortar Battery. Later they retired to the west side of the Quarry and dug cover. The attack had failed. Once more, the Battalion had, apparently, failed to carry through a definite piece of work entrusted to it, and once more it had only its dead to show for the effort and sacrifice expended. Yet the 2/5th should not be judged by the result of these attacks any more than its worth should be lowly appraised because of its inability to force the enemy out of Le Verguier. The truth is that, in both instances, it was given an impossible task to perform.

Eventually it took a whole Division to dislodge the Germans from these Farms. How then should four companies, each well under strength, accomplish the work without strong artillery support ? The strength and likely resistance of the enemy there had been very much under-estimated and many good lives thus sacrificed in vain. The casualties to the 2/5th in this operation were about one half of the attacking force. One hundred and fifty, all ranks, were reported killed, wounded, or missing. Out of a total of one hundred and fifty who took part in the attack on Cologne one hundred casualties were suffered.

On the 5th the Battalion were relieved and went back to support in Hesbecourt and Hervilly ; on the 6th it changed places with the 2/5th Battalion South Staffords, marched to Vraignes, and occupied billets vacated by them.

CHAPTER VI

PASSCHENDAELE

On the left of our attack, North Midlands and London Territorials, attacking both sides of the Wieltje-Gravenstafel and St.
Julian-Gravenstafel Road, also captured their objectives and beat
off a counter-attack.

—*London Daily Papers*, 27th Sept. 1917.

THE Battalion did not remain long in Vraignes.* On
May 15th, still remaining in Divisional reserve, it moved
up again to Jeancourt (one company) and Vendelles,
taking over from the 2/5th Lincolns who were billeted
in these places. At this time none of the 59th Division
were in the line, all units having been relieved by the
Cavalry Division during the past week.

The weather at this period was simply glorious, and, in
spite of the fact that working-parties had to be found each
night for work on the main line of resistance running
through Grand Priel Wood and east of Le Verguier,
there was plenty of time left over for resting and sleeping
and generally making billets and their surroundings more
homelike and comfortable. Concerts and sing-songs
were arranged, and on the 24th, two companies, " C " and
" D," and a company of R.Es. stationed near, held some
sports.

After a fortnight spent in this fashion the Battalion
paraded at 5 a.m. on the 29th and moved north by easy
stages (breaking the back of the day's march in the cool
of the early morning) to the Havrincourt Wood sector.
One night was spent at Hamelet and the next at Equancourt until finally, on the third day, the Battalion relieved
the 1/5th East Lancs in support at Metz-en-Couture

* A draft of 86 arrived from the Base and joined the Battalion
here on May 12th.

88

(3 companies) and Havrincourt Wood (1 company) in
trenches running through Q.20. a. and b, Q.21. a. and
posts in Q.15. b.* Effective strength at this time was 32
officers, 698 other ranks. Whilst in support the Battalion found night working-parties for the front line
battalions, improving Lincoln Avenue and Sherwood
Avenue and other adjacent trenches. On the night of
June 4/5th " C " Company, who were in Havrincourt
Wood, were ordered back to Metz and the following
night the whole Battalion took over the line from the
2/6th Sherwoods in the right sub-sector (Beauchamp).
Dispositions were—two companies in the front line Q.11.
b. 1.8 to Q.12. a. 5.5; one company in support at Q.11. d.
and one company in reserve in Intermediate Line Trench
in Q.17.

Here, No Man's Land was about 600 yards wide, much
too big it was thought, so the nights were spent in digging
and wiring advanced positions nearer to our friends, the
enemy.

It was in the No Man's Land of this sector that the
famous Boar Copse was situated, about which many,
most of them extremely legendary, yarns are told. Tall
stories of adventures whilst on patrol are to the army
what fishing stories are to the angler—a legitimate outlet
for imagination. If only half the things that were
reported really occurred at Boar Copse the Angels of
Mons should be relegated to the position of a mere pro-
vincial side-show.

On the night of the 11th-12th the 2/5th North Staffords
took over the line, and the Battalion marched back to
camp at Equancourt, the whole of the 178th going into
Brigade reserve at V.16 and V.11.

For the succeeding ten days intensive training of all
ranks was carried out daily, though a few working-parties
had to be found at various times. The weather was,
on the whole, exceedingly fine and hot, with occasional
heavy thunderstorms. The ubiquitous football made
its appearance and assumed its old-time place as first

* Reference Map 57 c. S.E. 1/20,000.

favourite among the men, even though the time *was* high summer. The *Crumps*, too, gave several performances to enthusiastic audiences.

On the afternoon of the 21st the Battalion marched to Dessart Wood (W.1. b *) taking over from the 2/4th Lincolns who were there in Brigade reserve.

Dessart Wood was a fairly pleasant spot. The Battalion lived in tents, and, except for the constant menace of working-parties by day and night, the men enjoyed the ten days spent there.

Working-parties and R.E. fatigues were, in the life of the infantry in France, what the poor are reputed to be in a civilized community, that is—ever present.

Fatigues differed in kind and degree. For an officers'-mess or cookhouse fatigue there would always be plenty of willing volunteers—especially if it kept a man off a battalion parade, or a route-march in full pack. The sort the men disliked were those that, in the shape of the orderly-sergeant, clutched a man suddenly, just as he would be settling down for a smoke or a quiet game of cards. At such a moment Private "Smith" could discourse fluently on the rottenness of army life and wonder loudly why he was ever such a fool as to join up.

But no battalion fatigue is comparable in the mind of an English Tommy to a R.E. working-party. He pretended to the fixed belief that the R.Es. were only in France in order to make work for the infantry. Certainly the only place a man ever felt safe from being detailed for a working-party was the front line. In support, or further back in reserve, men would get warned for duty under some casual cigarette-smoking sapper sometimes almost before they had got their packs off.

The map locations at which such sapper would have to be met would usually be some distance away at a dump. Here the men would file past and be loaded up with picks, shovels, sandbags, duckboards, beams and wire. Blessed was the sergeant on these occasions for, like the R.E., he carried nothing.

* Map Sheet 57 c. S.E.

Then, with the engineer leading and the sergeant bringing up the rear, the men would start, clanking, slipping, swearing, through endless trenches that caught their burdens in unexpected places, to their job. Little wonder, really, that men hated working-parties and usually preferred the comparative peacefulness of the advanced posts.

The old story of the sentry who, challenging a man, received the response " R.E.," replied in astonishment, " You can't be, you're carrying something," always went down well with an infantry crowd.

On the 28th a move forward was made in stormy weather to the Intermediate Line Trench east of Gouzeaucourt Wood. It was ankle-deep in water when the Battalion took possession.

Three days later the 2/6th Sherwoods were relieved ; "B" and "D" taking over the front line trenches east of Villers-Plouich from R.7. a. 3.6 to R.7. b. 8.3 whilst "A" and "C" Companies took over support in the sunken road at Q.18.d and R.13. a.* joining Beauchamp and Villers-Plouich.

The battle casualties during the month of June had been nil and the Battalion began this tour of duty with an effective strength of 39 officers and 741 other ranks, 7 officers and 73 other ranks having arrived during the month.

The trenches at Villers-Plouich were in very bad condition when taken over, but were very much improved during occupation by the 2/5th. The front-line posts were joined up, trenches were widened and deepened and fitted with duckboards. The wire was also completed and strengthened.

And now happened one of those unexpected tragedies of which the war was so full. At about 10 o'clock on the morning of the 8th, the Battalion Commander, Lieut.-Colonel G. H. St. Hill, was shot dead by a sniper. Both officers and men refused at first to believe the news that he was killed. The sector was such a quiet one and

* Sheet 57 c. S.E.

that particular morning little firing had taken place.

It appears that after breakfast he had been making his usual round of the line, this time with the Intelligence Officer of the battalion who were to relieve the 2/5th that night. In passing along a rather shallow portion of trench he had stopped, with that freedom from any personal sense of fear which was one of his most marked characteristics, to point out certain features to his companion, and was caught by an enemy sniper, being killed instantly.

Soon after dusk the Battalion was relieved by two companies of the 2nd Battalion London Regiment (Royal Fusiliers)—58th Division.

Carrying its dead chief, the Battalion moved sadly back to Equancourt (V.11. a) where it spent the rest of the night, marching on the 9th to a camping ground in O.33. d, near Rocquigny.*

Whilst the Battalion was on its way there, those who could be spared assembled at 3 p.m. at the little British cemetery at Neuville-Bourjonval, to pay final tribute, on behalf of their comrades and themselves, at the graveside of Colonel St. Hill. He went from among his men amid universal sorrow. In his passing the Battalion knew that it had lost not only a very true and faithful leader, but also a friend. His large genial presence and homely commonsense, his love of humour and fair play, had endeared him to the hearts of all the men, and their regret at his death was sincere and their mourning unaffected.

*   *   *   *   *

On arriving at the map location at Rocquigny the Battalion, now under the command of Major F. E. M. Donne, found little in the way of a camp to take over. True the R.Es. had been busy, and had got so far as to erect tin shelters to house the field-kitchens, and had, also, begun work on some baths, which, by the way, afterwards proved most useful ; but in the place where huts or tents for the men should have stood there still waved

* Reference map, Sheet 57 c. S.E.

virgin thistles and rank grasses covering ground plenti-
fully strewn with old shell-holes, as was soon discovered
when bivvy-sheets arrived and the sergeant-major
attempted to dress the lines.

Here, to the relief of everyone, steel helmets and box-
respirators ceased to be an essential article of apparel for
all occasions. The Division was now back for training,
and out of the zone where these twin bugbears were
necessary adjuncts, even when calling on one's friends a
few yards away.

Almost at once, that is with only an interval of a day
for cleaning up, training began. Squad drill, extended
order, bombing and miniature range practice alternated
as surely as ever these things did in the old days in
England.

On the 14th, Major F. E. M. Donne left us, to our regret,
to become IV Corps Burial Officer, Captain T. H. L.
Stebbing assuming command until Lieut.-Colonel H. R.
Gadd, M.C., arrived and took over on the 28th of the
month. July closed with the strength at 39 officers
and 716 other ranks. Casualties during the month being
2 killed and 10 wounded.

During the first three weeks of August, under the most
glorious conditions as regards weather, the Battalion
remained in camp near the Rocquigny railhead. In
addition to platoon and company training everybody
was put through a bombing course and threw at least one
live bomb. Brigade and Divisional field days round Le
Transloy, involving the taking and retaking of Star and
Treacle Trenches amid the burden and heat of long
summer days, alternated with night operations, ending
with an attack at dawn across old fighting ground on the
other side of " Silly-Sally " (Sailly-Saillisel).

The country from here back past Combles to Albert
was one vast area of desolate spaces. Evidences there
were aplenty to indicate the ferocity of the fighting there
in 1916, during the first Battle of the Somme. Everywhere among the wastes of shattered woods and débris
of villages the ground was littered with the aftermath of

war in the shape of unexploded shells, tangled wire, fallen-in trenches and shell-holes. Everywhere, too, isolated and in groups, wooden crosses reared their primitive heads to mark the spots where rested soldiers, British, French, and German, buried side by side where they fell. Also, beside the torn roads and bumpy artillery tracks, mounds humped themselves, a piece of wood stuck in them announcing to the uninitiated that there a horse lay under a light covering of earth.

At this time great attention was paid to the training of specialists, scouts, snipers, runners and Lewis-gunners. Scouts and snipers used to go off on mysterious errands of their own under Lieutenant Kane, and later, when he transferred to his old Battalion (1st Sherwoods), 2nd Lieutenant F. E. Andrews took the young idea in hand, and literally proceeded to teach it how to shoot.

Reinforcements began to swell the depleted ranks. On August 5th, 53 N.C.Os. and men arrived and were followed on the 18th by a second draft of 179. In some of these the men recognized old friends, back again after a few weeks or months at the Base, due to wounds or sickness.

Needless to say, games formed an integral part of the life at this period. By filling in shell-holes a fairly respectable field was obtained and many an exciting finish was witnessed.

Between the camp and Ytres, amid a circle of trees, were the remains of a farm known as the Four Winds Farm ; here with some labour, such as the filling in of crump-holes, etc., a course was evolved and a very popular race meeting was held. *The Cat* was a hot favourite, and, unlike many favourites, did not, on this occasion anyway, disappoint her backers, coming home first in the pack-pony race. In the Officers' Chargers Plate the Battalion mounts did not shine and we were all ashamed of them.

On the recreational side of life at Rocquigny must be mentioned the Divisional sports held at Barastre on the 21st. Inter-battalion boxing matches were also organized.

Another form of amusement, containing more than the
ordinary element of chance, was the Sherwood Cinema.
The men who ran it did their best, but sometimes the
fates were against them and the flickers would obstinately
refuse to flick.

During all this time the four companies had marched
in turn to Baulencourt (just south of Bapaume) for field-
firing practice. A good many thousands of rounds were
blazed away amid some of the hottest weather experienced by the Battalion on active service. Nor was it
only the weather that companies found sultry. One of
the butts was so sighted that the attendant markers were
unable to keep as cool as they would have wished during
bursts of rapid fire. In addition one luckless subaltern
remembers a very warm five minutes with the G.O.C.
Division. The General happened along with his G.S.O. 2,
ostensibly to see how the practices were going, but
turning suddenly on a poor second-lieutenant, waiting
to take his platoon forward to the firing point, he ordered
him to synchronize watches. For five terrible minutes the
platoon commander said " pip " at what he thought to
be the moment, only to find himself either a second too
late or too early. Finally the General gave him up,
doubtless as a hopeless case.

The Battalion at this period was well up to strength
in junior officers, and as the whole of the Battalion
officers shared a joint mess, and a very meagre one at
that, consisting originally of one small dilapidated wooden
hut, some very hilarious evenings were spent. After
dinner on wet nights, when there were no counter attrac-
tions optional, like *The Crumps* or the Cinema in the
Quarry, or obligatory, like "night ops," the tables and
forms were cleared out of the way and parlour games of
the more strenuous sort were indulged in, chiefly under the
direction of Captain Stebbing. Blindfold-boxing and a
game invented and christened the " great push," in
which the opposing forces, British and German, lined
each side of the Nissen, met in the middle of the floor at
the word " go," and strove each his hardest to press his

opponent back to the wall, were hot favourites. All very tame and poor-sounding now, but thoroughly enjoyed at the time, because leavened with the yeast of goodfellow-ship and happy comradeship and set in circumstances remote from all aids to amusement other than a worn-out gramophone.

After parades, during the light hours on fine nights, a riding school was established by the Colonel and enthusiastically helped by Major Trench. Aspirants to equestrian honours here learned at the feet of Lieuten-ant Whiston (Acting Quartermaster) and Lieutenant Spendlove (the Transport Officer) the gentle art of stick-ing on a horse with toes in and back straight.

But all this came to an end on August 24th, when camp was struck and the whole Brigade moved to the region of Albert, the first stage in their journey north, so rumour said, to take their share in the battle for Passchendaele Ridge.

By the aid of motor buses the journey was completed in one day. Early in the morning a long convoy of London buses lined the crooked street through the ruins of Le Mesnil-en-Arrouaise village and soon with clock-work precision the 2/5th and another Forester battalion had embussed and were on their way, via Le Transloy and Bapaume, to Le Sars. Here, lying in the fields off the road, was the other half-Brigade sleeping its after-lunch sleep and waiting to take our places in the buses. This was the halfway point and the rest of the journey had to be done on foot. The men found this march extraordinarily tiring, due partly to heat and dust, perhaps, and partly to the depression engendered by surroundings. For the route lay entirely across the old Somme battlefield. On every side were the remains of hamlets rendered historic by the homeric conflicts that raged for, in, and through them. Coming at last to the top of Thiepval Ridge, Albert Cathedral Tower, with its leaning virgin, burst into view. Before Albert and to the left was the famous crater of La Boiselle; below Crucifix Corner and Blighty Wood. On the far side of the valley the hutted camps at Aveluy could be seen in the evening light, and an hour later the Battalion marched into one of these (Bruce Huts),* very thankful to be there at last.

The Unit remained here exactly a week. During that time training continued over the disused trenches on the ground rising to Thiepval. But the training had a difference. In place of the old wave method of attack, where platoons and companies in extended order followed each other at intervals behind the barrage, a new formation was introduced. This consisted in men going forward in small bunches or groups at irregular intervals.

All this meant that everybody had to forget the old system practised at Le Transloy and Sailly-Saillisel and become, instead, so thoroughly conversant with the new method that, when they found themselves amidst the confusion and turmoils of an attack, they would act almost automatically along the lines laid down. This sudden change of tactics had been rendered necessary by the changes on the part of the Germans in their methods of defence. At Passchendaele they no longer held a series of trench systems, heavily wired, one behind the other at comparatively close intervals—these could be located and rendered untenable by artillery. Instead they defended in depth and held ground by isolated strong-points, farms and other natural places, well concealed and heavily concreted to resist artillery. One of these posts, well-sighted and containing picked machine-gunners, could hold up the advance, sometimes, of a whole division coming forward in waves of isolated individuals. Our "Blob" formation was the British High Commands' reply to this very effective change of defence on the part of the enemy. Its success in action is its answer to its critics. Our men working in small units, either as Lewis-gunners or bombers, were thus enabled to flank and outwit the occupants of the pill-boxes.

The great drawback to Bruce Huts was the lack of water ; every drop, both for cooking and drinking, had

* Reference Map. Albert continued sheet 1/40,000 W.16. a.

to be carried by water-carts from the water-point.
Against this there was the lake in Aveluy village, and
every day the men were marched there to wash or bathe
as the fancy took them. Everyone, too, made good use
of this return to civilization and shops, even if the civilians were few and the shops attenuated. Most evenings
were spent in buying picture postcards in Albert, visiting the estaminets, and, by the officers, at the Officers'
Club, where once more they saw tablecloths and were
waited upon by the fair hands of the opposite sex.

The Battalion now numbered 992 all ranks and was
stronger than it had been since its days in England.
It was stronger, too, in those other attributes which go
to the making of a soldier. Five weeks of intensive
outdoor training beneath an August sun, hard living and
healthy games showed itself in the lean forms, bronzed
faces and clear eyes of the men. They had been under
fire, had taken their part in more than one attack. In
their eyes could be read that quietness which the knowledge of these things brings to the sons of men. The
men began to look upon themselves as among those who
knew, as veterans and " old sweats " ; the Battalion
had been " bloodied."

So when, on August 30th, the news went round that
the Battalion would move in the small hours of the next
morning, men accepted the intelligence without emotion.
Everyone realized it to be but the preliminary to active
participation in the bloody struggle for the ridge before
Ypres. Yet no one worried very much or speculated
greatly about the future. All, by this time, were in
that quiescent frame of mind which came to most soldiers,
sooner or later, in France. Sheer boredom made any
change welcome, and for the rest, well that was in the lap
of the gods. If one's name were on a shell, well it was
hopeless to think of dodging it. It would get you
wherever you were, in the forward saps or back among
clean straw in the billets behind.

By 2.30 a.m. on the 31st everybody was aroused, hot
tea provided, and by half-past three, after hurriedly

KANSAS
CROSS.

THE
ENCLOSURE.

OTTO
FARM.

GALLI-
POLI.

SOMME
FARM.

AEROPLANE VIEW OF GROUND OF ATTACK. 26th Sept., 1917.   [See page 108

(Taken 15-7-17.)

GROUP OF BATTALION OFFICERS. (October, 1917.) [See page 121

Back Row: 2/Lt. Barrows, Lt. Whiston (Acting Quartermaster), Lt. W. Binks, Lt. Spendlove (Transport Officer), 2/Lt. Haig.

Second Row: Capt. Waterhouse (O.C. "D" Coy.), Capt. Swann (O.C. "B" Coy.), Lt. Williamson (Adjutant), Major Trench 2/Lt. Hall, Capt. Judd (Padre), Lt. Woolley-Smith (with "Betty"), Capt. Mearns (M.O).
(2nd in Command), 2/Lt. Andrews (Asst. Adjutant), Capt. Littleboy (O.C. "C" Coy.), Capt. Clifford (O.C. "A" Coy).

First Row: 2/Lt. Witt, 2/Lt. Gandy, Lt. Lavender, 2/Lt. Stone, Lt. H. Binks.

stuffing mugs into bulging haversacks, the men were on
parade before the first faint streaks of light appeared to
herald the coming of another day. The march to Beaucourt would have been a pleasant one under other conditions, but the night air cut keenly, and the men marched
silently, beneath the weight of their heavy packs.
Gradually, as the light increased and the dim shapes on
either side of the road showed themselves as familiar
objects—the wrack of war covered by nature's kindly
cloak—the men, warmed by marching, began to talk and
finally to sing. Those mysterious fears, that assail even
the most unimaginative during the still hours, were
dispelled by the new day. Youth and health asserted
themselves, and jokes and laughter floated up and down
the line. Who cared ? One was alive to-day and among
pals! Why worry about the morrow ?

The following lines, written by someone at the Front,
sums up the British soldier's philosophy in France, and
of our own Battalion in particular :

" DON'T WORRY."
THE WAY THE MAN AT THE FRONT LOOKS AT IT.

Of two things one is certain : Either you're mobilized or
you're not mobilized.

If you're not mobilized there is no need to worry ; if you are
mobilized, of two things one is certain : Either you're behind
the line or you're at the front.

If you're behind the line there is no need to worry ; if
you're at the front, of two things one is certain : Either you're
resting in a safe place, or you're exposed to danger. If you're
resting in a safe place there is no need to worry ; if you're
exposed to danger, of two things one is certain : Either you're
wounded or you're not wounded.

If you're not wounded there is no need to worry ; if you are
wounded of two things one is certain : Either you're wounded
seriously or you're wounded slightly.

If you're wounded slightly there is no need to worry ; if
you're wounded seriously of two things one is certain : Either
you recover or you die.

If you recover there is no need to worry ; if you die you can't
worry.

The train was ready in the siding at Beaucourt, and by
6 a.m. both men and transport were safely aboard and

H

the journey began. Back through Albert, past the old
camp on one side and the lake and Pozières Ridge on the
other, the train steamed with its human freight. Men
played " pontoon " or " nap," slept, ate their bully
beef and biscuits, or sat on the floor of the trucks, with
legs dangling, watching the pageant of life go by. Northward ever northward as they rode those bumpy trucks,
through stations like Amiens, Doullens and Hazebrouck,
they watched the blighted landscape of the Somme give
place to quiet villages, homesteads and pleasant fields
untouched, outwardly, by war.

At 4 o'clock the train ran into the little Flemish town
of Godesvaersvelde. Here guides from the advance
party met the Battalion and reduced its spirits to zero
by answering inquiries " how much further ? " with
" Oh, you've a hell of a march yet." A peculiar accident
happened on this train journey. The lower door (hinged
downwards) of a goods train passing ours, swinging to
the motion of the train, caught the legs of one of " C "
Company's men and flung him and another man, whom
he clutched, on to the permanent way. Both men were
severely bruised and one of them sustained a broken
limb, but luckily neither was thrown between the metals.

The march to the camp at J.2. a. 8.0,* near Winnezeele,
though only eight miles, seemed unending after a night
without sleep and a day in the train. The fellows pulled
themselves together as the column went through Steen-
voorde ; and later, as dusk fell, when the Battalion
halted in a village, drooping spirits revived under the false
hope that the journey was near its end ; the field-kitchens,
boiling gaily in rear, came forward to their various companies and a hot meal was served. It was not until
11.30 p.m. that, very sore and sorry for themselves, the
men spread their ground-sheets, rolled their blankets
around them and sank quietly to sleep, with the moon
shining through the white canvas above.

Waking the next morning the Battalion found itself
in surroundings remote from the concomitants of war.

* Reference Map.   Sheet 27.

The camp was sighted on the fresh grass of the paddock of a farm. Round the corner of the out-buildings was the kitchen-garden with its orchard beyond, all untouched by shell or trench. After six months' sojourn in devastated areas, civilians and estaminets now formed the background of the daily life. Milk, fresh eggs, butter and vegetables could now be had either from the farm or from the village or any of the cottages scattered across a landscape of standing crops.

Before this, in fact whilst the Battalion was still out training behind the Somme front, leave began to come through, and many a man, for no other reason except that hope springs eternal, began to, what was called, " sweat on the top-line."

But leave warrants for both officers and men dribbled along slowly in small batches at almost weekly intervals, so that most men took their dream of home with them into the hell beyond Ypres, where, in all too many cases, they were destined to lie for ever, buried in the dirty ditches of that much scarified ground. But a few were lucky and got it. Once more they saw their own folk amongst the villages and hills of Derbyshire.

There is, perhaps, no feeling akin in all the world comparable to the feeling that takes possession of a man going on leave. The fear that, even with the pass and warrant in his paybook, something will turn up to prevent his going after all, makes him anxious to get away from the vicinity of the Orderly Room, even before it is strictly necessary. The long walk (in full kit, tin hat, rifle, box-respirator and all), with occasional lorry-jumps to the railhead, brings the terrible thought that the train at Poperinghe may be bombed or an accident happen to it before it reaches the coast. In spite of incredible openings for misadventures, the train does arrive at Boulogne without mishap. After a night in the converted brewery or in the Rest Camp the boat is boarded, and a few hours afterwards he finds himself in a well-kept carriage, with doors and windows intact, running past trim hedges dividing fields where cattle and sheep graze peacefully, a world away from the wrack and tempest of war. Back for a time anyway among his own people, talking the same language, using the same money, thinking the same kind of thoughts. In a word, home. Thank God.

Going back is a different pair of shoes altogether. Returning with a leaden heart, the nearer one gets the more firmly does the machine grip one, especially if one be a Tommy. At home one is free to come and go. On the journey to Folkestone the same freedom is there. But once off the train men find themselves marshalled on to the boat, and, on the other side, lined up again and marched away to the Rest Camp. Officers, on the other hand, because there were less of them, were not so tied. At Boulogne they could either stay at the excellent Officers' Club provided or find their own accommodation at the many hotels in the town. There were, however, always a certain number of unlucky ones who clicked for duty on the boat, or, what was worse, found themselves detailed to march parties to the Rest Camp. Young subalterns on their first leave usually came in for these things. Others, following the adage " once bitten twice shy," became wary, and many were the subterfuges employed to outwit the Ship's Adjutant and his assistants.

Some would go down on to the lower decks and sit unobtrusively among the men until the danger had passed. Others would remove the tell-tale pips from their Burberry. In this connection a story goes that one subaltern, verging on middle life with his hair turning grey at the temples, removed the evidence of rank from his trench-coat and when approached said, blandly, " Oh, very well, but is it usual for majors to be detailed for work of this sort ? " Profuse apologies and hurried exit of captain in search of other prey.

But to return to Winnezeele. Contrary to expectation eighteen days were spent here and practically the whole of the time was given over to practising the new method of attack. Here the Yukon-Pack made its first appearance

and created great interest. Companies practised loading
and carrying these, but although excellent things in
their way, they never became familiar or of much use
to the Battalion.

On the 16th the Battalion, less the Lewis-gunners, were
taken by bus to La Ronville, where a short musketry
course was fired at the Fifth Army School of Musketry,
Mentque (Tilques). This practice was hurried through,
and on the 19th everybody was back in camp at Winnezeele.

The reason for this haste was soon made plain, when, at
six the next morning, the camp was evacuated and the
2/5th route-marched, by an indirect route, to Watou.*
The next two days were spent quietly in resting and
battalion sports.

On Sunday afternoon, the 23rd, after church parade in
the morning, the Battalion marched by Switch road,
north of Poperinghe, to "B" camp† at Brandhoek, on the
Poperinghe-Vlamertinghe road.

Brandhoek camp was one with dozens like it lining the
Ypres road. It was a mere collection of rat-infested
huts, none of which contained much in the way of comfort,
unless the few broken-down wire beds, standing forlornly
here and there, can be described as comfort. But the
outstanding feature of all these camps at this period
were the piles of tins and rubbish round the incinerators.
Unlike some of our allies who were more easy-going in
this respect, English army discipline was ever very strict
on the question of refuse. But here and in other camps
like it units had moved in and out, only staying, perhaps,
a few of the dark hours, in the feverish moves and
counter-moves of the game. So the Maconochie and plum
and apple tins thrown hastily on to the heap, by men
engaged in more pressing work, accumulated, and none
had time to deal with them in the orthodox manner.

Those whose luck it was to pass along the road between
Poperinghe and Ypres during the push of 1917, are little

* Map sheet Belgium 27. L.8. c. 35.
† Map sheet Belgium 28. N.W. G.6. d. 44.

likely to forget the experience. It was comparable to the traffic that swirls past the Royal Exchange, London, at high noon. Up and down the Ypres road, night and day, came and went a never ending, never slackening, stream of lorries, staff motor-cars, guns, ammunition columns, water-carts, field-kitchens, pack ponies and Lewis-gun limbers. Everywhere, too, were men ; in ones and twos coming back off leave, looking for particular units ; in small squads and in larger formations like companies, integral parts of yet more battalions moving up. In and out of this traffic went the swifter-moving motor ambulances, going up empty and returning in an unending stream with their agonizing loads of heroes. A fine white powder churned up by these human ants hovered continually over the road, covering everything, men, horses and vehicles, in a coating of dust. Men shouted the latest news or rumour as they passed : such and such an objective had been taken, or the —th Division had been cut to hell. And over all the guns (a little further up almost wheel to wheel) continued their never-ceasing chant, rising at times to a deep crescendo that shook and rattled the tin roofs of the huts as far back as Nine Elms and Poperinghe.

The 2/5th spent the 24th in final touches. Everyone made sure of his field-dressing and indentity-disc and all those many other articles lumped together as fighting kit. The plan of attack was explained to all ranks and final instructions given. Company commanders had visited the vicinity of the line the previous morning and had seen, as far as possible by day, the route they would have to lead their men by night.

At 6 p.m. the Battalion moved off. A certain number of officers, N.C.Os. and men were detailed to remain behind as a nucleus, and these with mingled feelings watched their friends march steadily away until they became lost in the flood of traffic on the road.

Once out on the Ypres-Pop. road progress was slow, and there were many halts. At last Ypres was reached and unconsciously the leading platoons quickened their

pace—fear always clung to Ypres although the sight
of some tin-hatted M.M.P. was somewhat reassuring
Salvation Corner past, the Battalion crossed the stagnant,
shattered canal, turned to the left along its northern
bank, passed some cosy dug-outs, when a sharp turn to
the right brought the companies on to No. 6 track which
led to Wieltje. We were not the only ones who wished
to use the duckboards at that hour; " Ethel " also
thought she would go along it, and nearing Wieltje, we
gave way to the lady—she was a tank.

It was past midnight before the old trenches at Wieltje
were reached and the 2/6th North Staffords relieved.

Here in rat-infested shelters the Battalion lived till
the night of the 25th.

The general plan of attack was this:

At 5.50 a.m. on September 26th, seven British divisions would attack on a six-mile front—from just south
of Tower Hamlets to north-east of St. Julien. The 59th
Division was one of those seven divisions, and it would
advance on a two-brigade front along each side of the
Wieltje-Gravenstafel road to a depth of approximately
2,000 yards, capturing a long line of hostile strong-points.
The Lincoln and Leicester Brigade would be on the right
and the Sherwood Foresters Brigade on the left: these
would pass through the Stafford Brigade who were
holding the line, the latter thus, automatically, becoming
brigade in reserve.

In the 178th Brigade the 2/6th and 2/7th Battalions
would capture the first two objectives (i.e. as far as the
Kansas Cross-Zonnebeke road). The 2/5th Battalion
on the right, and the 2/8th Battalion on the left, would
then pass through the 2/6th and 2/7th Battalions and
capture the third and final objective—the 2/5th Battalion Deep Trench, the "Enclosure" and Otto Farm;
the 2/8th Battalion Fokker Farm, Toronto Pill-boxes,
and Riverside.

Of the 2/5th Battalion "C" Company on the right
and "B" Company on the left, with "A" and "D"
Companies in support, would attack Deep Trench and

then "B" Company would capture the " Enclosure " while "C" Company would send forward two platoons to capture Otto Farm.

Besides a heavy bombardment of back areas, we were to have a creeping barrage of shrapnel, H.E. and smoke. It would travel at the rate of 100 yards in four minutes, with pauses of twenty to sixty minutes at the first and second objectives, and with a protective barrage, fired in bursts throughout the succeeding day, beyond the third. Otto Farm would be singled out for special attention, and would be given a " box " barrage of H.E. and gas all to itself throughout the whole attack, so that its garrison would be thoroughly fed up before "C" Company arrived. . . . .

As the final success of the 2/5th Battalion's attack depended on "B" and "C" Companies, Brigadier-General Stansfeld, D.S.O., had previously taken Captains Swann and Littleboy to Corps Headquarters, near Poperinghe, where on a contoured model of the Ypres Salient the actual lie of the land was seen and the attack explained.

By day the men lay low and rested. But when the sun began to sink and shone in the faces of the enemy, eyes cautiously appeared over the parapet and watched a demonstration 18-pounder barrage, arranged for Tommy's instruction, on the German defences. Later a flight of German planes came over and dropped bombs promiscuously. In the growing dusk the senior subaltern in each company went up to tape out the forming-up positions of their companies just behind the front line, while the companies themselves were busy dishing out bombs, flares and extra bandoliers.

At 11.30 p.m. the companies girt on their fighting order, looked to box-respirators ; wire-cutting men felt for the white tape on their left epaulettes ; Lewis-gun teams counted their slings.

Quietly the word was passed " lead on," and dim shadowy forms filed out of the trench and turned to the left along the fascined road that ran from Wieltje to

Gravenstafel.* "B" and "D" Companies followed this road past Spree Farm and Capricorn Keep to their assembly place while "A" and "C" Companies struck off right-handed to No. 5 track—a duckboard path winding in and out amongst the soggy shell-holes, with here and there a dead man or mule lying by its side. Now and again a gun flashed, lighting up for a moment the backs of the moving men, and a Verey light rose and fell, casting its brilliance over the shell-torn scene. Slowly the men moved along the track, the duckboards squelching under their weight, to Somme Farm. Here Mr. Haig of "A" Company and Mr. Robinson of "C" Company, showed the companies the line they had taped out earlier in the evening. It was now 2 a.m. on September 26th.

When the companies were at last settled in scattered shell-holes, the company commanders stumbled and floundered across to the road and down it to Capricorn Keep to report to the C.O., and synchronize watches. Here Battalion Headquarters would remain till the attack had begun, when, as soon as possible afterwards, it would move to Gallipoli. Picking up the various landmarks they had noticed on their way—the sickening smell that came from Somme Farm being their chief guide—company commanders returned to their companies.

And now the wait. . . . It is perhaps easy to be brave when there is something to be done, but to sit still in wet, cold shell-holes, all huddled together for warmth, with no talking above a whisper, is a nerve-racking experience.

At 3.50 a.m. our guns began the bombardment of the German lines. The area east of Ypres, where guns were almost wheel to wheel, was lit up by continuous vivid flashes ; shells went screaming overhead. Immediately came the enemy reply, making our men wonder whether this or the next one would land in their shell-hole. "B" and "C" Companies luckily had formed up just in front of the German barrage line, but "A" and "D" Companies had an unhealthy time.

* Reference Map. Gravenstafel 1/10,000.

The inferno lasted two hours. Then, just before zero our guns stopped as suddenly as they had begun : but only for a moment. With a throbbing roar dead on 5.50 a.m. our guns spoke again and our fellows knew the time had come.

Jumping up out of shell-holes, the N.C.Os. collected their men about them, and the advance began. Through mist thickened by H.E. fumes and smoke they looked weird figures as they stumbled forward across the tumbled ground.

It was a good barrage and the Battalion had but little work to do. A few isolated enemy posts and portions of deceased enemy were all they saw.

As day dawned the mist grew thicker and direction was very hard to keep. Our line of advance was roughly due east, but as there was reflected light in the west this was not much help. One officer was heard to announce in no uncertain voice that the line of advance " of course was over there " pointing to the light in the west. Maps and compasses were consulted, the swamp around Fokker Farm and the Kansas Cross-Zonnebeke road were located and the advance went on. Here Captain Swann and a few men of "B" Company extracted, with the aid of a Mills, eight or ten Germans from a pillbox just west of the road.

And now the mist cleared and our men could see Otto Farm and the " Enclosure " ahead. On the right were the Lincolns and Leicesters also moving forward. It was almost plain sailing. The enemy opened heavy fire both from Otto Farm and from low-flying aeroplanes, but the Battalion had fleshed its bayonets and would not be stayed. Creeping forward bit by bit, ably led by Mr. Binks and Sergeants Freeman, D.C.M., and Morley, "C" Company, now hopelessly mixed up as regards platoons, neared the Farm. Suddenly a red-cross flag was seen fluttering in the breeze. "C" Company rushed forward, and one by one the garrison was brought out. "B" Company meanwhile had firmly settled themselves in the " Enclosure " without much opposition.

The attack was over and the objectives won. Now came consolidation, the sorting out of men and preparations against a counter-attack which was sure to come. Prisoners were sent back in parties of twenty, each party in charge of a Tommy—Tommy in his element—tin hat awry, hands deep in pockets, rifle slung over shoulder, marshalling prisoners thankful to be still alive and ready to *kamerad* on the slightest hint.

How different the whole show had been from what one had expected! Formation had been impossible, and the advance looked more like a football crowd returning home across country, than an attack in blobs. With so much metal whizzing about, it was a marvel anyone was alive, and there had been many lucky escapes. Quite early in the attack a shell-splinter struck the buckle of a man's equipment, bent it double, pierced his tunic and shirt and was afterwards found in his trousers. A little later the same man had a bullet clean through his box-respirator from right to left and then a bullet just grooved his left shoulder by the epaulette. Fate had been kind to him.

Midday found the Battalion reorganized in a shell-hole position. Otto Farm and the " Enclosure " were strongly held and- linked up by a few posts. Deep Trench was never found—it had been completely blotted out—but near the place a shell-hole line was manned by men from "A" and "D" Companies. The companies were still mixed up, but the men were under their own N.C.Os. We were also in touch with the 177th Brigade on our right and the 2/8th Battalion on our left.

The sun came out—enemy shelling ceased—flares had been burnt—contact aeroplanes had klaxoned acknowledgment—the men rested. Haversacks were opened and their contents eaten. In the foreground Abraham Heights were visible, swept at intervals by a storm of shell-fire, our protective barrage. The men munched their bully and watched the impact of bullets from our barrage " Emma Gees," and watched shells go plonk into the marshy Hannebeke. The ground was so torn and shattered by shell-fire, that when a shell burst, even 200 yards away, men felt and saw the earth around them gently heave and settle.

At 3 p.m. some low-flying planes disturbed the serenity, and shortly afterwards the Lincolns and Leicesters and ourselves were shelled a little. Some figures, too, across the stream, began to move about as if in preparation for a counter-attack. But Lewis-gun and rifle fire hastened their movements to ground again and the shell-fire ceased.

At 5 p.m., when it was growing dusk, a regular tornado of shells burst upon our line. " There is evidence that our operations had anticipated a counter-stroke which the enemy was preparing for the evening of September 26th, and the German troops for this purpose were now hurled in to recover the positions he had lost." (Sir D. Haig's despatches).

As soon as our men saw the enemy approaching in force, the S.O.S. was fired and our barrage fell. At first the Lincolns and Leicesters had to bear the brunt of the attack, and were forced back, leaving the 2/5th Battalion in a precarious position with its right flank in the air ; so much in the air that "C" Company, with "A" and "D" Companies, became the front line and " B " Company support.

The garrison of Otto Farm fought stubbornly ; Lieutenant Binks, Sergeants Freeman, D.C.M., and Morley, Lance-Corporal Ford and Private Herbert being especially worthy of mention. But at last, to prevent themselves being entirely cut off, this garrison withdrew with the rest of "C" Company to the " Enclosure " where, with "B" Company, and "A" and "D" Companies on their right, a stand was made. And now in the growing dusk men could be seen advancing from what had been our right rear, but now was our right front. Germans ? Who knew ? As they came nearer our men could just make out in the uncertain light the British steel helmet—our counter-attack . . . the enemy was repulsed ; our line was again advanced to its former position, though

Otto Farm itself, which made a sharp salient, was not reoccupied.   Our line was once more intact.

Night fell.

The first care now was to guard against further attacks.   Our line was reorganized in depth ; rifles were cleaned.   The wounded were bound up and sent to the rear ; identity discs were cut off our own dead and papers were collected from the German dead.   This done the companies sought a little rest.   The night was cold ; the men were shelled periodically ; they longed for dawn.

At last it grew light (September 27th), and the strain became less tense.   Weird bully-beef-tin tommy-cookers were produced, tea mashed and rations eaten.

The Germans scarcely shelled at all till 4 p.m.   Then a most terrific storm of shell-fire smothered our positions. The ground shook, the platoons were covered with earth and the air became black with smoke.   In the midst of the tumult, Privates Bottomley and Crossley appeared, bringing some S.O.S. rockets from Battalion Headquarters.   It was a very fine exploit and deserved a higher decoration than the one awarded.

No counter-attack developed and the shelling ceased.

At 10 p.m. the 2/6th Battalion came up to relieve the Battalion and the 2/5th went back and settled in the area between Gallipoli and Keir Farms.   Slits were cut in shell-holes ; sentries posted.   Worn-out, our fellows slept the night away.

Throughout the 28th the enemy strafed at intervals, but not with any great severity.   It was the evening hate which was to come that our men dreaded.   Tea was mashed in good time—they had no mind to have that spoilt—that done and disposed of, they waited.   At 5 p.m. the hate began.   Those peering forward out of shell-holes saw the front line blotted out in a veil of writhing smoke.   Slowly the strafe came towards Gallipoli as the German gunners systematically searched the area.   Now it was on Kansas Cross, now on Kier Farm—nearer and nearer it came ;—it arrived.   The men and officers cowered in their shell-holes and shivered—their blood was not hot, they had leisure to think. In a quarter of an hour the guns lifted their fire and poured down on Gallipoli and beyond. . . . Once more men peered forth and watched the slowly drifting haze of dust and smoke.

As soon as it grew dark, each man rose from his shell-hole, yawned and stretched. The ration party was detailed and the rest of the men were employed on salvage work and burial of the dead.

Barely had the rations arrived and the rabbit-stew, steaming hot from food-containers, devoured, than the whistle and pop of a gas shell was heard. Gas masks were hastily pulled on. For two hours the bombardment lasted, and the helmets were a slobbery mess when finally removed, though a man in "B" Company found his so comfortable that he was discovered asleep in it at stand-to next morning.

In the afternoon of the 29th came the welcome news that the 2/5th were to be relieved that night by the New Zealanders. As the latter were not going to take over our positions, as soon as the evening hate was over, our men in small groups set off across country to the Wieltje-Gravenstafel road, along it, past Spree Farm, St. Jean and Salvation Corner and thence by a boarded track to the main Ypres-Pop. road once more.

Trekking along, all men's thoughts ran in the same groove. First and foremost, " What if I should be hit by a chance shell or bullet ? " a fear that grew in proportion as the danger decreased ; secondly, " What a blank long way. How blank heavy equipment and rifle are." But behind all thoughts dwelt the knowledge that the Battalion had at last *made good*.

Meantime Rear Headquarters had moved forward and occupied huts on the south of Vlamertinghe. On this night (the 29th) the company-quartermaster-sergeants and cooks had a hot meal and blankets ready, and guides went out on to the Vlamertinghe crossroads to wait for the Battalion.

There was a bright moon and the night-hawks were

busy, as they always were throughout these months, dropping bombs on roads, dumps and encampments. Continuously from dusk to dawn planes buzzed overhead, loosing their eggs in quick succession and racing away for more.

At a little past ten the guides sitting in the ditch a little way down the Ypres road saw, among the swirl of traffic, vague figures straggling slowly back in small squads. As they came nearer they became recognizable as men of the 2/5th. But what a difference ! Less than a week before, the companies had marched down this same road strong, bronzed and clean after months of preparatory training. And now all that was left of them, a mere handful only, covered with filth and half-dead with fatigue, laboured slowly back to camp. It was a heart-breaking sight and the like of which the old church tower at Vlamertinghe saw enacted night after night. Of the company officers, who took part in this attack, only four led their men back from the mudholes in front of Wieltje. "A" and "B" had only one officer left in each Company, " C " Company two, and "D" Company lost all its officers, either killed or wounded.

The following report on the attack by the Officer Commanding the Battalion is worthy of reproduction in full. It is interesting, not only as a further contribution to the records of this engagement, but also because it will serve to indicate the very real share Colonel Gadd had in its success.

The Battalion was always very fortunate in its Commanding officers. Colonel St. Hill's death had been a heavy loss and the men had marked his passing from amongst them with a deep sense of sorrow. They, almost to a man it was noticed, when writing home, deplored his death as an almost personal loss. In Colonel Gadd, Colonel St. Hill had a worthy successor. Fearless, without being silly, his object at all times was to get the most done with the minimum of discomfort and risk to all concerned. He thought continually of his men, and never spared himself in his efforts to appreciate every detail of any

operation in which the Battalion was about to take a
hand. Some indication of this will be noticed in the
concise, straightforward phrases of his report.

2/5th Battalion The Sherwood Foresters.

Secret.

REPORT ON OPERATIONS 26TH SEPTEMBER, 1917.

1. GENERAL.—On the morning of 26th inst. the Battalion under
   my Command attacked the enemy's position, in conjunction
   with the troops of 178th Infantry Brigade, and in accordance
   with the orders received from the Brigadier-General 178th
   Infantry Brigade. The rôle allotted to the Battalion was
   to support 2/6th Sherwood Foresters until their second
   objective had been reached, and then to pass through them
   and capture and consolidate the line of the Enclosure
   D.14. b. 4.4, D.14. d. 7.7. *Otto Farm* was then to be captured
   and held, and a line of posts was to be established on this
   general line.

2. DISPOSITIONS.—My dispositions were regulated by verbal
   instructions received from B.G.C. 178th Infantry Brigade,
   which entailed keeping one company as a reserve in its
   forming-up place and sending only two platoons forward to
   Otto Farm. I had previously determined that it would
   require two companies to attack and hold *Otto Farm*, but my
   plans had to be modified in accordance with the above.   "B"
   Company therefore was ordered to attack the Enclosure
   D.14. b. 4.4 and "C" Company to reach this line, and when
   the barrage lifted off *Otto* to attack it and hold it with two
   platoons, leaving the third to hold the line to "B" Company's right.
   "D" Company detailed one platoon to mop up for "B"
   and "C" Companies and the remainder were detailed as an
   immediate support to the two attacking Companies.
   "A" Company was retained as a general reserve about
   Aisne Farm.

3. APPRECIATION.—As *Otto Farm* was to be held I considered
   it important to ensure that the 177th Infantry Brigade on
   my right were fully cognisant of the fact and were prepared
   to establish a line of posts to protect its right flank.   On the
   afternoon of the 25th instant, I therefore sent my Adjutant
   to the 2/5th Lincs. Regt., to explain my plan and to impress
   the above point on them.   He did not consider that the
   arrangements they had already made were sufficient for our
   support and informed 178th Infantry Brigade Headquarters
   of the fact.
   The two Brigades concerned then succeeded in co-ordinating
   a scheme which would ensure satisfactory mutual support
   between the two battalions.

4. **ASSEMBLY LINES.**—Assembly positions were marked out in accordance with Brigade instructions, the front line of deployment being our line of emplacements D.13. c. 2.6 and my left being on the road. The depth of the Battalion was about 300 yards. "D" Company formed up behind "B" Company on left and "A" Company behind "C" Company on right. At 4 a.m., in reply to our preliminary bombardment, the enemy put down a heavy barrage and "D" and "A" Companies suffered considerable casualties.

5. **THE ASSAULT.**—At 5.50 a.m. the assault commenced and a general advance was begun. From the outset the Battalion experienced great difficulties in maintaining direction. The *Wieltje-Gravenstafel* road was very difficult to determine and compasses proved unreliable. The Battalion, however, succeeding in passing through 2/6th Sherwood Foresters to time and continued the attack. Very little opposition was encountered by my two attacking companies, but the greatest difficulty was still experienced in keeping organization and direction. The thick fog and the dust and smoke giving the attackers all the difficulties of a night advance.

The Enclosure was captured by "B" Company and Captain Littleboy, commanding "C" Company, collected his men preparatory to assaulting *Otto Farm*. As the two platoons detailed for this purpose appeared too weak, Captain Littleboy collected all the men of his Company.

6. **CAPTURE OF OTTO FARM.**—The Company advanced and got as close to the barrage as possible ; when it lifted the assault was delivered. A certain amount of opposition was encountered, but the place was bombed and most of the garrison ran out. Many were killed and about 40 prisoners were taken. Touch was made with 177th Infantry Brigade on right.

7. **POSITION AFTER THE ASSAULT.**—At 10 a.m. my situation was as shown on attached Map A, Captain Swann and the remains of "B" Company were holding the Enclosure and had pushed out a line of posts connecting it with *Otto Farm* which was held by about 15 men of "C" Company. The remainder of these two companies were either casualties or had lost their way and were not available for reserves. The whole of "B" Company had suffered very heavy casualties from shell-fire and all their officers had been wounded (N.B. This Company at the end of the day only numbered 28). Of those that were left, some had joined Captain Swann in the Enclosure, and others Captain Littleboy in *Otto Farm*. I therefore deemed it necessary to move forward to *Deep Trench* D.14. d. 1.9. This they had to do through a heavy barrage, and as they had sustained heavy casualties before *zero* their fighting efficiency on arrival was very small.

8. WITHDRAWAL FROM OTTO FARM.—Meanwhile Captain Littleboy had personally been to see an officer of the 2/5th Lincolns on his right and had arranged with him for the protections of his right flank. Shortly after this the enemy opened fire on the troops on his right, and they appeared to suffer heavily. They then withdrew about 500 yards, leaving his right uncovered. A defensive flank was then formed with a Lewis-gun and Captain Littleboy again went to the Battalion on his right and asked an officer why they had retired. He pointed out that *Otto Farm* was beyond their objective and he did not propose to hold that forward line. Early in the afternoon a small local counter-attack on *Otto Farm* was repulsed by rifle-fire from the farm. About 5 o'clock the enemy opened a heavy barrage along the front, and particularly against the 177th Brigade on the right and the counter-attack was seen developing from N.E. *Dochy Farm*. The retrograde movement of our troops in various parts could then be seen in progress and Captain Littleboy in *Otto Farm* could see the enemy to his right rear threatening "B" Company in the Enclosure and the line further to the left. With the objective of preventing the apparent rolling-up of the line the troops from *Otto Farm* were withdrawn by him and the line of "B" Company was prolonged and covered to the right. Just before it was dark, many of the troops who had retired returned, and the line was firmly established on the line of the Enclosure.

9. SUBSEQUENT PROCEEDINGS.—Little could be done in the way of reorganization during the night 26-27th as the situation was for a long time very obscure and it was considered more important for the troops of the Battalion, all of which were in the front line, to maintain the positions they were in. Further German counter-attacks were expected (N.B. the strength of the Battalion holding this line at present was 171). During the night stragglers were collected and a reserve of about 30 men was made near Gallipoli to which Battalion Headquarters had moved. About 4 a.m. on the morning of the 27th, as soon as it was practical to do so, this reserve was ordered forward to about *Deep Trench*, but as they were starting a very heavy hostile barrage was put down and their move was postponed until daylight, when it was cancelled. On the night of the 28-29th the Battalion was relieved by the 2/6th Sherwood Foresters and was reformed about *Gallipoli*, where it remained in support of the 2/6th.

10. GENERAL.—All ranks displayed at all times an offensive and soldier-like spirit and the men responded to every call made upon them. A number lost their way during the attack, but in practically every case I am satisfied they

joined up as soon as possible.   During the retirement during
the evening of the 26th some joined in, but the greater portion of them only retired on to the supporting troops two or
three hundred yards in rear and soon came forward to rejoin
their comrades.

Fifteen of them reached *Wieltje* and were returned on the
following morning, and a few were collected by me in the
neighbourhood of *Gallipoli*.

I am in possession of the names of most of those who went
past Battalion Headquarters and enquiry is being held into
their conduct.

11. HONOURS AND AWARDS.—The names of all those particularly
deserving of award are being forwarded under separate cover.

12. POINTS FOR CONSIDERATION.—In accordance with 178th
Infantry Brigade 688G. of the 1st October, I beg to bring
forward the following points :—

(1) It was very difficult to find the final objective and to
keep direction as stated in the above report.

(2) The Barrage was very suitable and troops could get
within 50 yards of it.   They, however, continually got
mixed up in it.

(3) Formations were suitable.   It was found very hard to
keep these formations owing to fog and smoke.   They are,
however, considered the most suitable.

(4) The dress and equipment was satisfactory in every way,
excepting that bombs should be carried in the side
pockets.

(5) Owing to the confusion during the first night, little could
be done for the comfort of the assaulting troops.

(6) This was not satisfactory.   Tapes should be put out at
least the night before, and the C.O. and company commanders given a chance of inspecting them.   It would
also be very useful if a map could be supplied showing 4
exact lines of enemy's barrage.   It requires watching
carefully for at least three days previous to the attack.
This can only be done satisfactorily by people living in
the line.

(7) For the front line shell-holes improved to shoot out of
appear to be the best.   No casualties were incurred by
the Battalion after the termination of the fighting in the
front line composed of shell-holes, although it was heavily
bombarded several times.

(8) If machine-guns are allotted to battalions they must
join them in time to march to the position of assembly.

Map A. attached.

(sgd) H. R. GADD,

Lieutenant-Colonel
Commanding 2/5th Battalion
The Sherwood Foresters.

Almost as soon as the remnants reached the huts, and were grouped round the field-kitchens eating the hot meal prepared for them, bombs were dropped on the camp. Luckily, in spite of many narrow escapes from flying splinters, no one was hit, although a number of horses were killed. The Staffords (who shared the camp with us) were not so fortunate. A bomb registered a direct hit on one of their huts and several casualties resulted.

The next day was spent in resting, cleaning up, and in checking rolls. There is, perhaps, no sadder thing than the reckoning after a battle. As name after name is called but without response, one or other of those fortunate enough to be left will give what information he can. Sometimes it can be stated definitely by a survivor that Private "Smith" was killed or was sent back wounded : the survivor was near him at the time. But mostly, the information forthcoming on these occasions is of the scantiest. "Jones" would be beside his pal at one moment, a shell would burst near, and when the smoke had cleared a little, "Jones" would be gone. In the turmoil and noise, amid the dust and smoke, men were too pre-occupied with themselves to notice very much what was happening around them. If a shell exploded among a group in a shell-hole it would more than likely wipe out the whole lot, and there would be no survivors afterwards to tell the tale.

Happily some of the men posted as missing this day were later traced through dressing-stations far afield behind other divisions, but all too many of the Battalion's finest lads went " out " from among their comrades without any certain knowledge as to the manner of their passing.

It is permissible to anticipate events and give here the List of Honours and Awards made to the Battalion in connection with the operation on the 26th. This list was published in Battalion Orders, November 7th, 1917.

EXTRACT FROM B.O. 7/11/17.

2. HONOURS AND AWARDS.
   The following awards have been made in connection with
the operations on September 26th last.

Military Cross.
Capt. C. N. Littleboy.
Capt. A. C. Judd (CD.)

Military Medal.
201164	Sgt. Morley, T.	C Coy.
201919	L/c Ford, R. H.	C Coy.
15347	Pte. Turner, A.	B Coy.
27584	Pte. Geeves, H.	B Coy.
11898	L/Sgt. Powell, J.	B Coy.
6409	Sgt. Lawson, C.	D Coy.
201945	L/c Collier, H. J.	A Coy.
202125	Sgt. Harpham, H.	D Coy.

The following also have been awarded Cards of Commen-
dation by the Divisional Commander :
202370	Pte. Bottomley, F.	C Coy.
202415	Pte. Crossley, W. C.	C Coy.
201991	Pte. Downs, T. S.	B Coy.
202543	Pte. Kingston, J.	B Coy.
22857	L/Sgt. Lane, J. (Died of wounds).	

CHAPTER VII

CAMBRAI

It was now that Bonaparte made his first effort to baffle the science of those who fancied there was nothing new to be done in warfare.

—BOURRIENNE, *Memoirs of Napoleon.*

EARLY on the morning of October 1st, to everybody's great joy, the Battalion left Vlamertinghe by train for Steenbecque. Detraining there at one o'clock a comparatively short march brought the Battalion in early afternoon to the straggling village of Les Ciseaux.* Here in lofts and barns amongst clean hay and straw the men settled for a few days.

Only those familiar with the Salient will realize just what this meant. The Salient was ever synonymous with hell in the mind of the British Tommy. Especially so was it during the summer and early autumn of 1917. Even as far back as Vlamertinghe and Poperinghe the days were never free from shelling, nor the night from continuous and heavy bombing.

To lie peacefully on one's back on the grass in the orchard with no sound to break the stillness, except the foraging of the hens in the yard or the squeals of the pigs anxious to be fed, seemed, by contrast, like a touch of Paradise to our boys.

Although many a heart was heavy at the thought of the pals left behind for ever amid the shambles of *Wipers*, youth asserted itself as youth must, and at eventide as dusk fell, happy voices, raised in laughter and song, floated out from cosy billets along the roads about Les Ciseaux.

During the day there was much to do. Clothing

* Reference Map sheet 5a Hazebrouck 1/100,000.

boards were held, kit deficiencies noted and replaced, rifles and Lewis-guns thoroughly overhauled.

On the 3rd the whole Brigade, which was by now concentrated in the area, was inspected at Boeseghem by the G.O.C. 178th Brigade.

On the 5th the Battalion left Les Ciseaux in buses for Therouanne station where they debussed and marched to Delette.*

Delette was a somewhat dank little village in the bottom of a valley. The early autumn rains had turned its badly-kept roads into quagmires and added dampness to the discomfort of its somewhat unsavoury billets. A draft arrived on the 7th and was inspected by the Brigadier on the following day. The householder at the Headquarters mess discovered himself as an enthusiastic photographer, and, taking advantage of a temporary gleam of better weather between the showers, he photographed the officers and sergeants on the grass before his front door.

On the 10th the Battalion began its trek south, and once more, towards the line. The first night was spent by " C " Company at Aumerval and by the others at Bailleul-les-Pernes ;† starting at 11, the men were not billeted till after dark.

The following morning the march was resumed at nine and was a short one, Camblain-Chatelain † being reached at 10.20. As a matter of fact, the Battalion arrived too early, and had to wait for some time beside the road outside the village, to give the 2/5th Lincolns time to get clear of the billets.

The late afternoon of the 12th saw the men housed in long French huts in a wood in the left of the hill running up out of Hersin-Coupigny.†

The Battalion was now in the heart of the Bruay coal area. To the miners among our lads (and there were many) the mining villages passed, and the miners themselves, coming back from the shafts in their pit clothes and shiny hats, were an interesting and homelike sight,

* Reference Map Sheet 5a. † Reference Map Sheet Lens 11.

and many a cheery remark was shouted by the fellows as they marched by them.

The next day the trek was completed, the Battalion being billeted in outbuildings and in part of the Château itself, at Gouy-Servins.* This château had been a remarkably fine and extensive place, fronted by a large courtyard lined with trees. All round the courtyard were stone stables and barns. Both these and the deserted house were filled with tiers of rabbit-wire beds able to accommodate several battalions with ease.

Almost directly, the 2/5th had to provide large working parties of 200 at a time for work at Souchez, evidence itself, to anyone inclined to doubt it, that the Unit was once more within the zone. These, a march to Carency for bathing, a demonstration in riveting by the R.Es. at Lens Junction, eked out by P.T. and Bayonet Fighting, filled in the days spent at Gouy. In spite of its nearness to the line, civilians still lived at Gouy, and the estaminets were crowded every night by our men spending their pay on *œufs*, bad *vin* (*blanc* and *rouge*), and still worse French beer.

On the evening of the 21st, the Battalion relieved the 2/4th Leicester Regiment in the Avion sector just south of Lens.† This sector was part of that portion of the line previously held by the Canadians. Naturally, therefore, the area immediately behind the trenches was covered by a complete light-railway system. The Decauville was always found in any sector where the Canadians made any prolonged stay. They raised this method of taking up supplies and evacuating wounded to a fine pitch of excellence and efficiency. It meant not only that rations, duckboards and wire were taken up to the trenches with greater expedition and a less expenditure of fatigue on the part of troops, but it also meant that the roads behind were far less congested by traffic in the small hours than many another and less busy part of the front.

* Reference Map Sheet. Lens 11.
† Reference Map Sheet 36 c s.w. 1/20,000.

Accordingly, on this occasion our Battalion was transported by Decauville from Gouy to La Coulotte. Many hours of long marching in heavy kit was thus obviated and the men arrived in the line fresh.

The sector, the Battalion now found itself defending, is perhaps second only to Ypres in interest to the British.

From Gouy the road winds up and then down into the Souchez valley. Down this ravine at one time meandered the Souchez brook, but this had, by this period, been almost obliterated. In pre-war days the valley must have been one of the beauty spots of a beautiful country ; days when the villages of Carency and Ablain St. Nazaire yet nestled under the shadow of the Lorette heights, while further up, on the lower slopes of gaunt Vimy, the little hamlet of Souchez sat snug and comely among her woods, watching the tourist go by on the main road from Arras to Lens and Bethune.

But Souchez, as our lads saw it, carried no trace of her past. The valley was filled from end to end with the wreckage of war. Not a house or a tree stood anywhere intact ; hardly a square inch of ground was unscarred by shell-fire. Only part of the tower of Ablain church remained, pointing like an accusing finger upwards towards Notre Dame, upon whose sullen heights the bones of many *poilus* bleached.

Before Souchez, Vimy rears abruptly. In years to come, when nature and man together will have put the world to rights again, visitors will stand in a new Souchez, and looking up at Vimy Ridge will try to picture it as the soldiers saw it, and lived in and about it, at this time. They will too, doubtless, try to visualize, first the French, and then the British soldiers crouching low in filthy holes and ditches in this veritable valley of death, with an ever-watchful enemy on the heights above looking down on their positions. And, finally, visitors will stand aghast at the colossal and almost super-human task, successfully accomplished by the Canadians, of taking this enormous ridge by direct assault. The story of bravery, sacrifice and dogged determination displayed in that Homeric conflict will never be told in all its fulness, for words fail to describe the magnitude and glory of that achievement.

The opposite side of Vimy Ridge slopes just as suddenly to a table-land which stretches away towards Douai. Avion is, or rather was, for nothing remains of it, a small village just off the main road between Lens and Arras and about two miles in front of Vimy. Our line ran from Loos down through the outskirts of Lens (Lièvin) and so on through Avion, Maricourt, round Arras towards Bullecourt. This represented the advance across the Douai Plain won at the Battle of Arras six months previously. The tangible results of that operation were that the great bastion Vimy fell into our hands, Arras was freed by the rolling back of the Germans from her gates and Lens rendered untenable as a railhead to the enemy.

In Avion the main line of resistance, Avion Trench, ran through the ruins of the village. It was well supplied with deep dug-outs kindly constructed by the Germans. In front of Avion and parallel to it ran another trench, manned by isolated Lewis-gun posts by day. At dusk this trench was properly garrisoned, and listening posts pushed forward from it into shell-holes and cellars. It was not a nice bit of line at all. The front was difficult to determine and from a high railway embankment the Germans commanded our line and plastered it at intervals day and night with trench-mortars. There was no wire in front of Sullivan, our forward trench. To erect entanglements there would have been a very windy business. No Man's Land was filled with the débris of collapsed houses, and the quietest patrol found it impossible to move far without dislodging loose bricks, which crashed away in loud advertisement of its presence.

On the 24th Avion and Cyril Trenches were heavily shelled by 4.2s and almost obliterated. They were cleared again during the night.

The following night, the wind at last being propitious,

" O " Special Company R.Es., from emplacements behind, projected gas drums on to various targets in the
neighbourhood of the Fosse, N.20. d. 2.2, N.33. a. 8.2, and
N.33. 6.2.6. All troops east of the Blue Line " Adept "
were warned to wear box-respirators and, as a further
measure of precaution, the posts in Sullivan sap. N.33.
a. 20.25 * were withdrawn thirty minutes before zero.
Divisional and heavy artillery co-operated by a preparatory shoot, followed by a raking barrage at zero.

Zero was fixed for 11 p.m. and all ration-parties were
warned to be clear of the area east of La Coulotte before
that hour. Contrary to expectation there was no retaliation by the enemy and no rockets were sent up. The
word " Opera " was the agreed signal for all clear but
the barrage died down and no message came through.
Companies began to get anxious. Finally, after one company had worn its respirators for five hours, it was ascer-
tained that Brigade had forgotten to send out the code
word. All the next day the pungent smell of the gas
hung about our forward saps.

The night afterwards the news was circulated that the
Intelligence, by intercepted messages, had information
that a raid was contemplated on our front. The whole
Battalion stood-to.

After midnight heavy firing broke out on our flank and
at 1 a.m. news was sent round to the companies that the
raid was taking place against the battalion on our right.
By 1.30 the raid had been repulsed, and the remainder
of the night passed without incident.

On the evening of the 27-28th the Colonel, who was not
satisfied with the dispositions taken over from the
outgoing battalion, reorganized the defence in depth.
This was accomplished by the fortifying and garrisoning
of three well-chosen strong points across our sector. One
was named " Cassius," and was situated in the centre
of Avion village. It was a cellar beneath a house that had
fallen about it like a house of cards. A platoon from
" C " Company occupied this. " B " Company garri-

* Map Sheet 36 c s.w. 1/20,000.

soned Battalion Headquarters at T.3. a. 4.1. which was
also turned into a strong point and named " Balbus."

Battalion Headquarters moved in consequence to the
sunken road at T.2. d.2.9, and took up their quarters in
dug-outs near the Regimental Aid Post, reached, as
many men will remember, by a camouflaged trench from
Beaver.

The following day, as if the Germans knew all about
the move, Battalion Headquarters was heavily shelled
by 4.2s.

The winter was now beginning its first tentative
advance and every precaution was ordered to prevent
loss of man-power by the malady known as trench-feet.
In previous winters thousands of men had gone down
the line in some cases almost permanently crippled with
this complaint. Soldiers living for days and nights on
end in the slime and muck of soggy trenches, without an
opportunity to remove their boots or change their wet
socks, found their feet gradually losing all sense of feeling;
flesh went dead and slowly turned black. A pin stuck
into the foot would not be felt though later the most
intense agony supervened.

In order to prevent wastage of men, stringent instructions were issued to all units. Trench-feet became, not
only a crime in the man, but a crime in his platoon
commander, and a slur on the good name of the
battalion.

Each day every man had to take his boots off and rub
his feet vigorously with oil under the personal observation of an officer.   Socks were changed every day.
Each night dry socks came up regularly with the rations
tied up in labelled sandbags.   Each night, too, the day's
wet socks went back in sandbags, labelled by platoons,
to be brought up again dried another night.   This
meant that each man had three pairs of socks in use, but
it was worth it.   By this simple method trench-feet was
practically stamped out.   Only those men who had
suffered from it before succumbed, and the number of
forms (in many colours) dealing with their case, that

these took down the line with them, were calculated to keep their luckless officer awake for many nights.

On the 29-30th the 2/7th took over and the Battalion moved back to Red Support. This tour of duty, especially after Ypres, appeared to be, and had been, a very peaceful one. Two casualties only were reported, both men unfortunately killed by a direct hit from a shell. In addition to the reorganization of the defensive system, the Battalion also left its mark in this sector by founding and naming a dump near B.H.Q. The name was invented by Lieutenant F. W. Smith (Battalion Signalling Officer) and sounded like the phonetic rendering of the sound made when sneezing. The word was " Houshmi," but to most men this became " hush-me," so " hush-me " the dump became.

The eight days spent in Red Trench were very pleasant ones. There were plenty of fine deep dug-outs full of tiers of wire beds. No shells fell anywhere near and on most days the sun shone. What more can a soldier ask ?

At night, though, the R.Es. took their toll, and working-parties were provided for improving and duckboarding Adept, Balsam, Beaver, Cyril, and La Coulotte Trenches. A draft of 62 men had arrived on the 26th from the 12th Sherwood Foresters—a Pioneer Battalion —and were wonderful fellows, especially on piece-work tasks definitely set them.

On the fourth of November a small party of picked officers and men quietly withdrew to Souchez. Information was wanted by the staff, and for this prisoners are useful. The best and quickest way to get prisoners is to walk across to the German lines and take them. In other words a raid on the enemy lines was contemplated, and the 2/5th was ordered to carry it out.

For this purpose plans were carefully prepared ; the spot where the crossing was to take place carefully reconnoitred. At Souchez the relative dispositions of the opposing trenches were constructed from aeroplane photographs and the scheme practised.

On the 8th the raid was carried out on Metal Trench

N.33. d. 20.70, and N.33. d. 45.53,* but was unsuccessful. The whole scheme rested on the blowing of a gap in the enemy wire by means of a bangalore torpedo. Surprise, daring and speed were the subsequent factors necessary to the completion of the plan. Unfortunately the men entrusted with the torpedo lost it in their progress across No Man's Land. Their story was that, floundering among shell-holes and débris in No Man's Land, the torpedo slipped from their hands. A long search afterwards by officers and men, among the long grass and weeds around the spot indicated, failed to find it, and eventually, for that night at least, the raid had to be cancelled.

Meanwhile two days previously the Battalion had been relieved by the 2/6th South Staffords and had spent the night trekking slowly back through Glucus communication trench, up Vimy Ridge and down the other side to huts at Souchez.

A week was spent here in the usual way, cleaning up, church parade, and bathing by companies at Carency. The camp was of the poorest and much time was given to its improvement. There were also the usual working-parties to be found for work in the line.

On the 12th, at the Château de la Haie, the ribbons of decorations and awards to officers and men for their share in the operations of September 26th were presented by G.O.C. Division. Only those to whom the awards were given attended, much to the regret of the remainder of the Battalion, who would have liked to have been present to cheer the distinction of their friends.

It was expected that on the 14th the Battalion would move up into the line again, this time into the left (Liéven) sector. During the week company officers had gone up there on reconnoitring expeditions to have a look round preparatory to taking over.

But life in the army is always full of surprises, and on the morning of the 14th the Battalion was paraded and, instead of turning to the left on the Bethune-Arras road, turned right and began marching south. Why?

* Sheet 36c S.W.

Rumours immediately began to fly : everyone had his theory and everyone tried to air it. But none knew. The Colonel may have known, but he kept it very quiet if he did. Someone announced our destination to be Verdun. He had seen this mentioned in a message and was sure. That night the Battalion found itself in huts, surrounded by several inches of mud, in the village of Agnez-les-Duisans. The name of the camp was Verdun, but it was hardly the Verdun the prophets expected. Late in the afternoon five days later, the Battalion, still wrapped in mystery, left Verdun camp in heavy weather, and arrived at Blairville at 9.30 p.m.

Again men asked each other where were they going and why were they moving by night ? Only essentials were unpacked that night and the next day, after three quarters of an hour's physical training, the men stood ready to move at an hour's notice.

Later the same day the veil was lifted; company commanders were sent for by the C.O. and were informed that a big push had begun that morning at Havrincourt, in which some hundreds of tanks had taken part. Further, the Guards and the 59th had been detailed as Divisions in reserve for this attack. Company commanders looked at each other. So that was the secret, was it ? Another push and the 2/5th to take a share in it. Well, they were glad to know. It was to be hoped the Battalion would be lucky anyway.

Orders to move at dusk arrived, but were afterwards cancelled. But the following night the Battalion marched through the rain to Gomiecourt and, arriving there at 1 a.m., found a few tents in the middle of a muddy field, and had to make the best of things with these.

At 11 a.m. on the 23rd, the Battalion marched to Bihucourt West and entrained at noon ; detraining at Fins the same day it marched to Equancourt and once more found itself in familiar surroundings. The news that came through was splendid. The enemy had been taken completely by surprise. A break through on a large front was reported. Cambrai had fallen! The war was over, boys : well, perhaps not quite, but very nearly.   We had them on the run at last.

The next day the C.O. and the company commanders reconnoitred the freshly-captured ground near Ribécourt, and were much interested in all that they saw.   Things really did seem to be going well in spite of the fact that the weather was still extremely wet.

Here the men bathed ; company training was carried out and inspections held just as if the German lines were pierced any day of the week.   Whilst here the Colonel and company commanders rode up through Dessart Wood to Beauchamp, passing many squadrons of dismounted cavalry waiting, as they so often did unfortunately, for that magic word which would send them riding off into the blue, after a hurrying and disgruntled enemy.

On the morning of the 26th the 2/5th moved to Marco-ing, arriving there at teatime.   Through Gouzeaucourt it went with the band playing gaily.   In the light of after events it is probable that this was the last allied band to play through Gouzeaucourt for many a weary month.   At Marcoing the staff had billeted the Battalion in a large factory.   But when the Colonel arrived he had everybody out and into cellars, and only just in time, for the enemy began to shell the town with 5.9s.   The front line was only about a mile away, yet few seemed to realize it, for already men had got the idea that the Germans had become a disorganized rabble straining desperately backwards in an endeavour to lose touch with the triumphant foe.   However, the next morning, realiza-tion that things were not going as they should dawned as a possibility to some ; the Battalion was suddenly ordered back to Equancourt and moved at two hours' notice.   It left by platoons at quarter-of-an-hour inter-vals, full of forebodings, which odd scraps of news about a Guards' reverse at Bourlon only deepened.

Thus at a stroke wild optimism gave place to an equally wild pessimism.   Since the push began nothing was too impossible to believe in the way of success, and now nothing was too improbable to be believed of defeat.

GROUP OF BATTALION SERGEANTS. (October, 1917.) [See page 121
Sitting: C.S.M. Perrons, C.S.M. Broomhead, R.Q.M.S. Ward, R.S.M. Cope, Major Trench, C.S.M. Tomlinson, C.S.M. Reader-Blackton.
Front Row: Sergeants Lawrence, Duckering, Warren, Taylor, Clark, Morton.

"CASSIUS" STRONG POINT—AVION SECTOR.

[See page 125

From now on for many days our men lived in a constant
atmosphere of strain. Rumours began, gathered mo-
mentum, flourished exceedingly, then faded away
and died ; but no one really knew anything for
certain. One day the Battalion would move back, the
same night it would be ordered forward again. Moves
and counter-moves following each other in rapid and
bewildering succession, till the senses reeled and men
wondered what was to come of it all.

From Equancourt on the 29th the Battalion moved
up into support at Trescault, south-west of Ribécourt
L.20. d. 5.3. The following morning it was reported that
the enemy had broken through at Gouzeaucourt and was
marching on Metz, and the Battalion, at fifteen minutes'
notice, moved east in extended order to Highland Ridge,
taking up a defensive line on high ground at approximately L.32.b. Central, where, on arrival, patrols were
sent out to get into touch either with our men or the
enemy. Daylight brought the welcome news that the
enemy advance had been checked. The Guards, the
story went, helped by the 59th Divisional R.E. Field
Company, and stragglers, such as cooks and American
light-railwaymen, had driven the Germans out of
Gouzeaucourt and back on La Vacquerie. This story of
the part played by the R.Es. in this engagement was
undoubtedly true and was extremely praiseworthy, for
Sir Douglas Haig later paid tribute to their gallantry
in a despatch. " In this operation the Guards were
materially assisted by the gallant action of a party of the
29th Division who, with a company of North Midland
Engineers, held on throughout the day to a position in
an old trench near Gouzeaucourt."

At dusk the Battalion was ordered back to support
line by Trescault, the K.S.L.I. taking over. During the
early part of the evening, owing to information received
that Marcoing had been evacuated, one company was
hurriedly sent to cover the Ribécourt-Marcoing road.

For the next three days the 2/5th stood-to, ready for
any emergency, in the old Hindenburg front line.

K

Orders were issued for the relief of the 2/5th North Staffords, but were afterwards cancelled. On the 4th our men moved back to the old English front line by Bilhem Farm.* Whilst here enemy aircraft dropped bombs on the Battalion area but only one man, luckily, was injured.

Early in the morning " D " Company had disappeared suddenly to Hermies, only to return as suddenly the same evening. Men were getting used to these lightning changes and almost ceased to wonder what was happening and where. The following day, a day of hard frost, in response to sudden orders, the Battalion moved up to fill a gap created in the line south-east of Flesquières. The march proved a nervy one. The guide, as so frequently happened, knew precious little about his job. He took wrong turnings and got the column down wrong roads and finally kept it standing for three-quarters of an hour whilst he thought the matter out. The Germans were shelling the area consistently, and the Battalion, waiting in fours on a well-defined road, did not feel particularly elated at the enforced halt. Two of the horses, indeed, took fright and bolted with the G.S. waggon, containing the tools, straight for the German lines.

Eventually, in the small hours of the morning, the companies reached their destination and found themselves in the not very envious position of linking up the division on their left with the unit on their right : both flanks were under cover in trenches. Company commanders were informed that Bourlon Wood was being evacuated and that the troops holding it would fall back through the Battalion just before dawn.

Thus with barely three hours to spare the men set to work to dig trenches and to erect entanglements : no easy task in ground hardened by frost. But everybody realized that their lives depended on getting under cover before daylight and, somehow, the job was accomplished, barbed-wire and all. " C " Company, acting as a screen, captured two prisoners who walked innocently into them.

* Reference Map Sheet Moeuvres (special).

It is difficult to say who were the most surprised, captives or captors.

Meanwhile Battalion Headquarters had established itself in a German dug-out just in rear. Here on this night, snugly below ground, Tragedy put forth its hand and touched it. The story is told so vividly and well in Captain Littleboy's book, that I cannot do better than quote the passage:

" Whilst hard at it with barbed-wire and pick, we noticed a huge column of black smoke with flames rising from somewhere behind us. Putting it down in our mind as nothing more nor less than a dump, we took no notice of it. Presently the smoke gave way entirely to sheets of bright red flame, and we realized then that the fire was not so very far away, and also in the direction of Battalion Headquarters. At last, determined to see what was happening, two of us hurried over to investigate. Columns of flame were seen pouring up from the Battalion Headquarters' dug-out shaft, five or six signallers were digging furiously at the mouth of another shaft which was hopelessly blocked up, whilst a second party of men were tugging for all they were worth at the arms and clothing of Major Trench, whose body was being slowly wriggled through a hole in the ground almost too small for its passage. After a short struggle he came out like a cork from a bottle ; a runner followed in like manner, coughing and spluttering and almost overcome with the smoke and fumes, that were now pouring up after him. Shortly afterwards this shaft was like the other, a sheet of flames.

" It was thought at the time that everyone had escaped, but too late it was discovered that two men were missing. Two days later Captain Stebbing went down at considerable personal risk to see if anything could be found. At the bottom of the dug-out he found two little piles of metal buttons and shoulder-titles—silent witnesses of a very pathetic tragedy.

" I believe the fire was caused by a petrol tin full of paraffin—not water as was supposed—being put on a stove to boil, with the result that the dug-out was a roaring furnace in a very few seconds.

"Some idea as to the narrowness of the occupants' escape and the heat of the fire can be gathered from the fact that, as Sergeant Warren, the last man to come out by way of the main shaft, was going up the steps, part of his tunic was burnt and two rounds of ammunition exploded in his pouches."

In addition to the loss of two valuable lives all orderly-room documents and records were destroyed.

The 6th passed quietly enough. One half-hearted attack by the Germans on our left flank (where the line was in process of being withdrawn) was easily repulsed. The night was spent digging posts and the same work was continued on the nights 7th and 8th. At 7 p.m. on the 7th Captain Swann, O.C. "B" Company, and Mr. Jackson were killed by a direct shell-hit on their head-quarters. Captain Swann was an admirable company commander, capable and efficient. Both he and Mr. Jackson were sincerely mourned by the whole Battalion, officers and men alike.

On the night of the 9th, "A" and "B" Companies were relieved by the 14th D.L.I., "D" Company by the 11th Essex. "C" Company and 8 Lewis-gun teams were left behind to man the outpost line from Beetroot Factory to L.13. d, b and c, about 300 yards out in No Man's Land, and came under the orders of the incoming Battalion for one night. To add to "C" Company's chagrin at being left behind, the frost broke and rain fell in torrents. The newly-dug trenches were quickly water-logged and the night pitch dark. Interest centred on rations, which arrived at last, in a terribly squashy condition—but, at any rate, safely. The code words for the completion of occupation by "C" Company were "None nicer"; the code word for the completion of the relief of the other companies was "Much better": "C" Company *was* furious.

On being relieved the three companies spent the rest of the night digging a communication trench—a continuation of Station Avenue between the front line and support, so " C " Company really did not miss very much.

The Battalion meanwhile had taken up its quarters in the Catacombs at Ribécourt.* These were weird and wonderful, and spacious enough to get lost in ; from them " D " Company moved the next evening to their old friend Unseen Support at K.35. b. just as " C " Company marched in. At 3.15 a.m. the following morning the rest of the Battalion joined " D " Company. The four days spent here were filled with real hard work. The line which had been in a state of flux, once more appeared to approach stability. The enemy counter-stroke had apparently beaten itself out and the strain was appreciably lessened. Winter had set in and days and nights were cold. Trench-shelters had to be made, trenches dug, deepened and drained, many yards of wire had to be reversed by dragging it bodily from rear to the front of trenches. Over and above all feet had to be rubbed assiduously.

On the 15th " B " and " C " Companies had a welcome break from the monotony of working-parties. They marched back to Lechelle for a bath, found they had already passed the baths on their way, near Neuville, and had to retrace their steps. The following day the right-half Battalion marched back for the same purpose, " B " and " C " Companies relieving them.

On the 18th the Battalion moved to trenches running from K.34. a. and b, to K.35, relieving the 2/8th Sherwoods. Whilst there a party working at the wire in No Man's Land (north-east of Flesquières) had two casualties during the night of the 19th.

The following day " B " Company was relieved by the 7th Border Regiment and was followed, three days later, by the remainder of the Battalion joining " B " at Baulencourt on the morning of the 23rd.

The Battalion was now out for its second divisional rest. Like its first, it came out to it from the Somme, but, unlike its first, it was, luckily, not to spend it there.

* Reference Map Sheet 57c.

For on Christmas Day the whole Battalion entrained at Bapaume with very thankful hearts. Later in the day it detrained at Petit Houvin and marched to Houvin-Houvigneul.* Appropriately enough snow fell during the day and Boxing-Morning saw the fields round the billets at Houvin covered thickly by snow. The billets were nothing, as the men said, " to write home about," but they were rest billets and straw and sacking went a long way. Thus ended Christmas Day, 1917. Men remembered the same festival a bare year before. To them it seemed longer than that away ; so much had been crowded into twelve short months ; so many gaps had been cut in the ranks ; and so many pals full of the wine and enthusiasm of comradeship and youth lay scattered somewhere under that carpet of snow, sleeping their last sleep amongst the wreckage of whole provinces.

This was the last Christmas of the war proper, though nobody could know that then. Had our fellows crowd-ing the dilapidated shelters at Houvigneul known it, Christmas Day might have been a happier day for some. Yet it was perhaps well those lads could not foresee the future. For the coming months were to be full of terror and despair, death and capture, heroism and sacrifice, for most of the cheery lads playing " Pontoon " and " House " round the braziers that night.

* Reference Map Sheet Lens 11.

CHAPTER VIII

BULLECOURT

All that was left of them—left of six hundred.
TENNYSON : *The Charge of the Light Brigade.*

FROM Boxing-Day till the end of the year the Battalion
was engaged in the peaceful process of snow clearing.
Snow fatigue, interlarded with many a mimic battle,
became the order of the day. Parade grounds had to be
cleared for training ; roads had to be cleared for traffic.
" B " Company even went so far afield as Doullens,
starting in the middle of the night, to clear the railway
line of snow.

Christmas Day, which had been spent in the train, was
celebrated on the 27th in the usual English fashion.
That is, everyone grossly overfed himself, then became
somnolent until pulled together by a first-rate concert
later in the day.

From now onwards to the middle of March the days
were filled with all varieties of training; battalion, company, and platoon, taking their turn with bombing,
bayonet fighting, saluting and physical drill. Subalterns suddenly found themselves remembered by Brigade,
and had whole days set apart for their special enlighten-
ment in the shape of tactical exercises.

Once a week the Battalion bathed and once a week
divine service was held.

On the 6th the frost gave suddenly, rain began to fall,
and soon the whole world—the soldier's world anyway—
became one vast sea of mud.

Work was eked out, of course, with sports. Many
afternoons were given over to football. A series of inter-
company matches was arranged, though the records

are silent on the results of these.   Long distance runs—
one of which (organized by Brigade and included all
officers below the rank of major), to Magnicourt, Gouez
and Manchoure, caused much heart-burning amongst
those whose rank had not kept pace with their weight—
and inter-platoon relay races were also arranged. A boxing
competition, too, was held on the afternoon of the first of
February.   Whilst, among the unofficial recreations,
must be mentioned ratting round the huts and, on more
than one occasion, fox hunting.

The first fox hunt came about in this way.   The
Transport Officer dug out and captured a fox.   His staff
collected all the stray dogs they could find and, carrying
Reynard safely in a sack, both dogs and men repaired to
open country.   Giving the fox a sporting start, hounds
and huntsmen were soon in full cry.   But the snow made
heavy going and from rising ground the breathless
chasers saw the fox leading the dogs, an easy winner by a
long distance.

These fox-hunts were immensely enjoyed by Lieutenant and Quartermaster, afterwards Captain, J. Farnsworth.   But apart from this, one excellent story is told
against him, whilst at Houvin-Houvigneul.   Here, as
a compliment to his large and genial presence, Madame
used to call him " *mon petit garçon.*"   One day the
Brigadier called in search of him and asked for " *mon
gros ami.*"   " *Mon petit garçon* ? " queried Madame.
" *Non, non,*" said the Brigadier, " *mon gross ami, mon
ami, comme ça,*" describing a tremendous semicircle.
Madame smiled to show she understood, but still stuck
to her " *petit garçon.*"   Few will forget his rum-punch,
which was a famous brew second only to his celebrated
" corpse-revivers."   But happy, jolly, companionable,
his own spirit was more splendid than either.

Of course, inspections were not forgotten.   The
Colonel inspected the companies on various occasions.
On the 19th the Divisional General reviewed the Bat-
talion and transport, and, early in February the G.O.C.
VI Corps, General Haldane, inspected the Brigade.   The

Medical Officer also had an inspection all to himself.
It may only be a coincidence, but shortly after this last
parade, a Foden steam lorry arrived and all blankets
were fumigated. The Battalion was again inoculated
during this period.

Lectures on Fire Control, Trench Routine and other
subjects were also given.

To help complete the reconstruction of the activities
of the 2/5th whilst in divisional rest, reference must be
made to one-day's leave to Amiens granted to some of
the men. A percentage of the Battalion had visited
Amiens on leave a year before when the Unit was out at
Rocquigny. On that occasion it necessitated a lorry
ride to Achiet-le-Grand, where a civilian train completed
the journey to that Mecca of so many British soldiers in
France. There was always great competition for Amiens
passes, and for very obvious reasons—it took a man
back, for a few hours at least, to the land of shops, pretty
girls and restaurants. Simply to walk up and down the
main street of Amiens jostled by the throng on the Rue
des Trois Cailloux, stopping here and there to look into
picture shops or book shops, was a joy that made the long
journey there in a dusty, bumpy lorry, a mere thing
of no account. Men entered shops and paid exorbitant
sums for small souvenirs and other articles they really
did not want, solely for the pleasure of spending money
or as an excuse to talk to a girl—any girl—behind the
counter. After months among devastated villages and
shell-holes these fighting men had it in their hearts to
envy, momentarily, the staff officers and others on Base
jobs to whom Amiens was an everyday event.

Amiens, at this time, was a gay, happy place, untouched
by the ravages of war. The Germans had been there
once in the early days and, in the months to come, they
were to be within an ace of being there again. How
near the world now knows. For, only six short months
later, Amiens was to be like a city of the dead : its
brilliantly lighted shops and tea-rooms closed ; Charlie,
so obliging (at a discount) when an officer wanted a cheque

changed, fled with his bar (so famous for its cocktails) to Abbeville ; the pretty girls in their dainty, tiny shoes, scattered to Trouville and Paris ; whole streets to lie wrecked by shell-fire, tram-lines rusty, wires to sag, forlorn and broken, about the roads ; the great glass roof of the railway station to be shattered in a million fragments, but, wonderful to relate, the cathedral to remain practically untouched. . . .

At the end of January a draft arrived, made up of men from the 2/8th Battalion, which had been split up under the reorganization of brigades on a three instead of four Battalion basis. The Battalion was very pleased to welcome these men to its ranks. Everybody sympathized with the 2/8th at thus losing its identity, but, circumstances apart, the 2/5th secretly felt that the draft ought not to feel so very sorry for itself. Things might have been worse, for it wasn't every man who got drafted to such a splendid crowd.

On February the 8th, the Battalion packed up *en route* for Bullecourt : divisional rest was at last at an end, and our men were once more to test their luck in the line. The move was carried out in easy stages, nights being spent at Boisleux St. Marc (Durham Camp) and Mory North.* Bullecourt was reached on the night of the 11th and the 18th Welsh Fusiliers and the 10/11th Highland Light Infantry relieved in the line.

Whilst on this trek (at Mory) a further small draft of thirty-eight other ranks joined from the 17th Battalion.

The Peace of Brest Litovsk and the liberation of thousands of troops from the Russian front, led experts to forecast a big German drive this spring. The Army Intelligence, which was, as a rule, extraordinarily good and correct in its information as to enemy movements and intentions, also expected a big attack as soon as the weather permitted. All along the line preparations went forward for meeting it, come when it would.

As everyone now knows the offensive came in March, the Bullecourt sector being one of the points over-

* Reference Map Sheet Lens II.

whelmed in the first onrush of the German storm-troops.

It is of historical value therefore to give here, in as great a detail as possible, the measures taken by our own Battalion Command to meet that attack. The following extracts from Operation Orders dealing with the defence of this sub-sector, issued under date February 5th, 1918, will be read with more than usual interest :

No. 56.
5/2/18.

OPERATION ORDERS

by

Lieut.-Colonel H. R. Gadd, M.C.
Commanding
2/5th Battalion, the Sherwood Foresters.

Reference Map—*Cherisy.* Special Sheet, 1/10,000.

1. INTENTION.—The Battalion will take over the trench sector now held by Right Front Battalion of the 119th Infantry Brigade, near *Bullecourt,* about the 10th inst.

2. DISPOSITION.—(a) The front line system will be held by 2 companies, " B " on the right, and " D " on the left. These companies will be based on the *Valley Support Line* and will find garrisons for the posts comprising the front line. The dividing line in the Support Line will be U.20. d. 8.4.

(b) " C " Company will be in support and will be situated in *Man Reserve.*

(c) " A " Company will be in reserve in *Railway Reserve.*

(d) Battalion Headquarters, snipers and wiring platoon will be in *Railway Reserve.*

3. LEWIS-GUNS.—The front line companies will each have 2 Lewis-guns in the line of posts and 2 in *Valley Support.* There will be 1 Lewis-gun in each *Trident* and *Vulcan* posts. Support and reserve companies will keep their Lewis-guns in hand.

4. SCHEME OF DEFENCE.—In case of attack the front line posts and *Valley Support* will be held at all costs, and companies in *Valley Support* will be prepared to form a defensive flank along *Pelican Lane* and *Jove Lane.*

The support company will be prepared to counter-attack across the open should the enemy penetrate any portion of our line, and will also be prepared to form a defensive flank along *Queen's Lane* should the front of the battalion on the left be penetrated. This company will counter-attack without orders from Battalion Headquarters. The reserve company will be prepared to counter-attack across the open and if necessary to form a defensive flank along *Pelican Avenue.*

A determined enemy advance must also be delayed by tenacious resistance in *Man* and *Railway* Reserves.

5. ADMINISTRATIVE ARRANGEMENTS.—(*a*) Front line companies will cook in *Valley Support* and support and reserve companies in *Railway reserve*.

(*b*) Water in tins will be sent up with the rations each night. By day it may be brought from *Ecoust*.

(*c*) A sock drying-room will be established near Battalion Headquarters. Dry socks will be issued from here and *not* from the Q.M. Stores.

(*d*) Whale oil will be drawn from R.A.P. daily.

6. DRESS.—Hairy and great-coats will be taken into trenches. Haversacks will not be taken, but will be left at Q.M. Stores filled with spare kit.

7. R.A.P.—The R.A.P. will be in *Railway Reserve*.

RIGHT SUB-SECTOR.

In continuation and supersession of Operation Orders No. 56 para. 4 and Instructions No. 1 para. 2.

1. DISPOSITION.—(*a*) The front line system consists of *Valley Support Trench* covered by a line of 12 posts about 300 yards in advance. The posts are numbered from right to left commencing with No. 1.

The front line system is sub-divided into two sectors, each held by a company.

(*b*) The support company is located in *Man Reserve*.

(*c*) The reserve company and Battalion Headquarters are located in *Railway Reserve*, about U.26. c. 2.6.

2. ACTION IN CASE OF ATTACK.—In case of attack the Battalion may be considered under two headings :

(*a*) Garrisons of certain lines and localities which must be held at all costs, no matter what the situation is, or to what depth the enemy has penetrated.

(*b*) Counter-attack formations which are used either for instant counter-attack on the initiative of their immediate commanders, or for a more premeditated attack under orders of the Battalion Commander.

3. GARRISONS.—The following will be held at all costs in accordance with para. 2 (*a*) above :

LOCALITY.	GARRISON.	STRENGTH.
Line of posts ⎱ *Valley Support* ⎰	Right and Left front companies.	2 companies.
Man Reserve	Support company	1 platoon. 1 Lewis-gun.
U.20. c. 7.9.	Support company	1 Lewis-gun.
No. 13 Post *Railway Reserve* U.26. c. 2.6.	Reserve company	1 platoon.

LOCALITY.	GARRISON.	STRENGTH.
No. 14 Post *Railway Reserve* U.26. c. 0.8.	Wiring platoon	1 officer and 36 men.

4. COUNTER-ATTACK.—The forces available for counter-attack will therefore be :

(a) 3 platoons less 1 Lewis-gun section of the support company.

(b) 3 platoons of the Reserve company.

Of the above (a) will be for immediate counter-attack on the initiative of the company commander, whilst (b) will only act under the orders of the Battalion Commander.

5. DEFENSIVE FLANKS AND SWITCHES.—Should any portion of the front be penetrated, the commander on the spot will immediately attempt to localize the enemy's success by forming a defensive flank, and manning the switch lines.

It is impossible to lay down definitely what troops would be available for this duty, but they should, if possible, be taken from the garrisons, thus leaving as many as possible of the counter-attack formations available for their allotted functions. It may, however, be necessary to utilize counter-attack troops for this, and the officers commanding support and reserve companies will make themselves acquainted with the flank defences and switch lines they may have to man. The most likely lines in this case are *Pelican Lane* and *Pelican Avenue* on the right, and *Jove Lane* and *Queen's Lane* on the left.

6. ANTI-TANK DEFENCE.—In the event of an attack by hostile tanks, arrangements have been made for dealing with the tanks with our artillery, and our rifles and Lewis-gun-fire should be directed at the enemy's infantry, which would be following to make good the ground gained. Lewis-guns in *Valley Support* have been issued with armour-piercing S.A.A. which should be used should the tanks reach short range.

7. ANTI-AIRCRAFT DEFENCES.—Anti-aircraft Lewis-guns will be mounted as under :

LOCALITY.	BY WHOM FOUND.
Battalion Headquarters.	Reserve company.
Man Reserve.	Support company.
Valley Support (2)	Front line companies.

All these guns are available in the case of an infantry attack.

Later, about the 15th, a further Lewis-gun post was established at the bottom of the valley at the junction of Golliwog Lane and the front line, and another in Valley Support at U.20. d. 73.88 commanding the valley running north-east.

The snow and the subsequent thaw had played havoc with the trenches, and practically the whole of this tour of duty was spent in repair work and improvements of defensive posts against the threatened attack. Night after night working-parties, of from 230 to 280 strong, were supplied.

On the 14th an inter-company relief was carried out, " A " Company relieving " B " and " C " relieving " D " Company. " B " became reserve company in Railway Reserve and " D " Company went into support at Man Reserve. This change over was carried out without untoward incident, although the front line was heavily shelled between 8 and 9, and 10 and 11 p.m. The code words announcing same to Headquarters, " Army Beer," were duly 'phoned through.

The night of the 17-18th saw the 7th Sherwoods in possession and the 2/5th back at North Camp, Mory. Here, as in the old days at Ypres, German airmen became most offensive and pressing in their attention. Bombs were dropped in the vicinity of the camp on several occasions, but, luckily, never quite on it.

During this rest-week the Battalion bathed at Mory, found large parties for digging at Noreuil and other places, spent endless hours on fatigue work improving the camp, was inspected by the Medical Officer, and generally employed its time in the usual way fashionable among the P.B.I.

Even here nothing was left to chance, and orders were circulated in case the promised offensive took place whilst the Battalion was out resting.

Owing to possibility of an attack by the enemy on the Brigade Front, and in order that the Battalion may be ready to move forward at a moment's notice, the following orders are issued :—

1. The Transport Officer will arrange to have four limber wagons permanently at North Camp, Mory. The limbers will be allotted one to each of " A," " B," " C," and " D " Companies. These limbers will report to company commanders to-morrow morning at 9.30 a.m. and will be available for the carriage of Lewis-guns and ammunition for same.

2. The Transport Officer will arrange for horses as under to be at the Camp within twenty-five minutes of receipt of code word " *Hun.*"

    (i) 8 horses for limbers as mentioned in para. 1.

    (ii) 3 officers' mounts.

3. In the event of orders from Brigade being received to move forward, the undermentioned Officers are detailed to proceed as under :—

Captain Clifford	Brigade Headquarters.
2/Lt. G. R. MacDonald	Battn. H.Q.'s of front line
2/Lt. H. E. Barker	battalion.

On the 23rd February the 2/5th relieved the 2/6th Sherwoods, this time in the left sub-sector. Orders were issued accordingly.

Reference Map *Cherisy.*

Special Sheet, 1/10,000.

1. INTENTION.—The Battalion will relieve the 2/6th Battalion, Sherwood Foresters, on the night of the 23-24th February.

2. DISPOSITION.—(*a*) The front line system will be held by 2 companies, " D " on the right, " B " on the left. These companies will find garrisons for the posts comprising the front line.

The dividing line between the front line companies will be *Knuckle Avenue.*

(*b*) " A " Company will be in support and will be situated in *Stray Reserve.*

(*c*) " C " Company will be in reserve in *Railway Reserve.*

(*d*) Battalion Headquarters will be in *Railway Reserve.* The signal section will take over the positions as at present occupied by the 2/6th Sherwood Foresters.

(*e*) The wiring-platoon will be accommodated by the reserve company.

3. LEWIS-GUNS.—Lewis-gun positions will be taken over as at present.

4. SCHEME OF DEFENCE.—In case of attack the front line posts and *Bury Support* to be held at all costs. The right-front company will be prepared to form a defensive flank down *Mars Lane* and *Queen's Lane,* and the left-front company down *Hump Lane* and *Hump Support.*

The support company will be prepared to counter-attack across the open should the enemy penetrate any portion of our line. This company will act without orders from Battalion Headquarters. The reserve company will act only under orders from Battalion Headquarters.

5. R.A.P.—The R.A.P. will be at *The Knuckle.*

6. DRESS.—Hairy and great-coats will be taken into the trenches. Haversacks will not be taken into the line but will

be left at Quartermaster's Stores under arrangements to be notified later.

7. COMPLETION OF RELIEF.—Completion of relief will be reported by code words as follows :

        " A " Company :   " *Mabel.*"
        " B " Company :   " *Interpreter.*"
        " C " Company :   " *Soap Suds.*"
        " D " Company :   " *Queenie.*"

This sub-sector included the famous Tunnel Trench. This tunnel, a beautifully constructed work, ran a long distance, so it was said, from somewhere near Arras in a south-easterly direction.   It was not used by the British and its entrances were blocked up.

Large parties continued to be requisitioned for work on communication trenches and Stray and Tiger Trenches. Each night, at least two patrols were sent out from both front companies.   On the 28th the Commanding Officer, Adjutant and company commanders of the 25th Northumberland Fusiliers reconnoitred the line, preparatory to relief by them on March 2nd, when the 2/5th went back to camp at Mory South.   Snow fell heavily during the relief.

The appearance of the 25th Northumberlands was due to a change in the organization of garrisoning the line. Previously all three brigades in the Division had held portions of the line at the same time, each having one battalion in reserve at Mory.   Under the new arrangement complete brigades were withdrawn in turn to reserve, thus simplifying matters considerably—especially for brigade staffs.   The Sherwood Foresters was the first Brigade to be withdrawn under the new system.

The seven days were filled with all-night working-parties (every third night at Noreuil), camp improvements, training, a test stand-to, and in reconnoitring tracks, dumps and routes.

On the night of the 10-11th the 2/6th North Staffords were relieved by the 2/5th in the right sub-sector of the right-brigade front, i.e., Vraucourt Noreuil.*   The tour was a quiet one.   Our artillery was very active (the

* Reference Map Sheet 57c N.W.

LENS—ARRAS ROAD (note Tanks parked on right).

[See *page* 128]

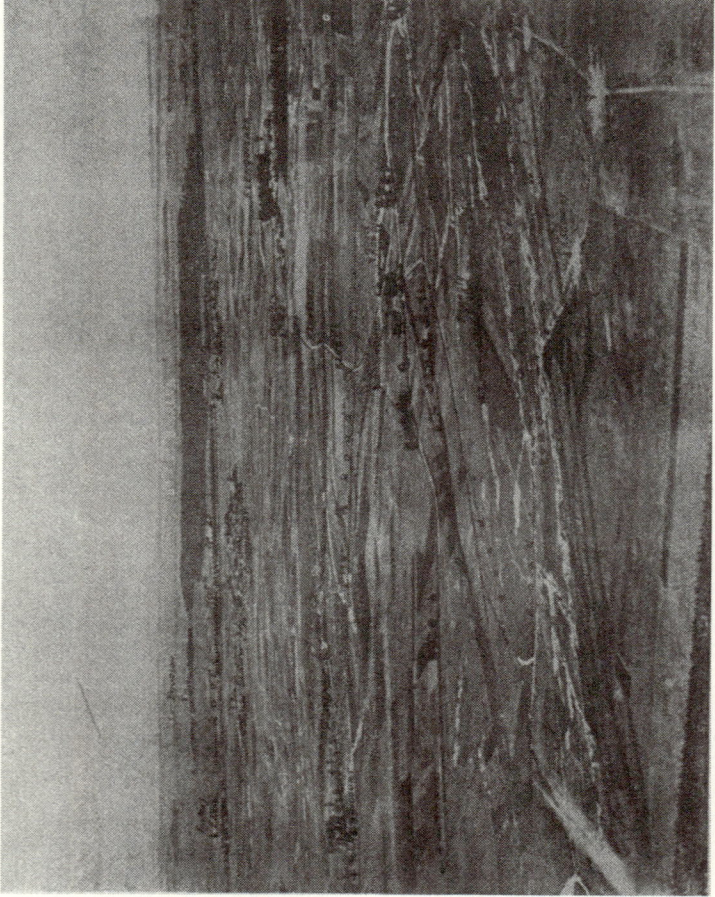

BOURLON WOOD AND FLESQUIÈRES.

[See page 132

infantry in the front trenches thought excessively so), but
the Germans remained for the most part quiet and did not
reply. " J " Special Company Engineers projected gas
on to his positions, without retaliation.

With the offensive imminent, it behoved all battalions
to watch enemy movements with extra care. Each
battalion constructed its own " O Pip " and the brigade
observers did likewise, and chose the best site. From
" Eagle's Eye," the Brigade " O Pip," a wonderful view
could be obtained of the country around Hendecourt and
Riencourt just behind the German lines.

Often we read in the " Daily Lie," " eight men seen
carrying planks or duckboards near the cemetery in
U.10. d, several times during the day," or " Smoke seen
from the cellar in U.10. d. at 9 a.m. and 2.25 p.m.," or
" three Germans wearing soft hats and without equipment carrying dixies in U.10 d. at 1 p.m." It was always
" U-ten-don "—so much so that at last an 18-pounder
was ordered to work in connection with " Eagle's Eye."
The observers used to wait till the enemy got well into
the open near the cemetery and then sent the tip to the
waiting gunners. A report—the shrill scream of the
shell—some Germans fell, some ran . . . and then the
smoke from the shell-burst drifted away.

But this never lasted long. Two or three shells—and
the enemy went to ground for the rest of the day. He
only came out again in the semi-dusk—that fateful
quarter of an hour when the unwary thought it was too
dark for the sniper.

The attack was expected at dawn on March 13th, so
from 2 p.m. on the 12th far into the night (those who
slept near a battery of 6-inch Hows. will testify to this)
the enemy was strafed. The area around Hendecourt
and Riencourt, the Crow's Nest and the Dury road were
in a haze of smoke from bursting shells, and now and
again coloured lights shot out in all directions as some
dump went up. And never a shell in retaliation for
such a pasting. We thought that G.H.Q. Intelligence
must have been wrong and that the Germans had not

L

many guns in the sector with which to reply. . . . Yet Intelligence was right—1,000 German guns fired on the Bullecourt front on " Der Tag."

On the 17th the 7th Sherwoods took over : the Battalion proceeded to Brigade support on the Ecoust-Noreuil road.

Thus on the morning of March 21st, the 59th Division held the front line of the right flank of the VI corps round Bullecourt. The 178th Infantry Brigade held the right-forward-sector, with the 7th Sherwoods on the right, 2/6th Sherwoods on the left front, and the 2/5th Sherwoods in support immediately north of the village of Noreuil.

The 2/5th were disposed in trenches and the sunken road in the neighbourhood of Igaree Corner at C.10. c. 6.9. Battalion Headquarters was in the sunken road running from Noreuil to Longatte approximately at C.9. d. 8.5.

At about 4.30 a.m. the enemy began a heavy bombardment on the whole area with gas shells. The alarm was immediately given, masks put on, and the companies moved out to their stand-to positions as follows :

Right-front : " B " Company to Noreuil Switch round C.5. c. 4.4.

Left-front : " A " Company to Sidney Avenue round C.4. d. 8.0.

Support-company : " D " Company to Pontefract and Dewsbury Trench round C.10. b. 7.4.

Reserve-company : " C " Company to Sunken Road round C.9. d. 8.5.

At 5 a.m. the bombardment increased in intensity and the gas-shells gave place to H.E. This was some relief to the men who had been fumbling about in the dark in respirators.

It is very difficult to reconstruct the true history of that fateful morning. All records, war diary, defence schemes, and operation orders were lost. The only immediate information available were one or two early messages which got through from the Battalion to Brigade Headquarters by runners (all wires were cut early by the shell-fire), and the statements of the four men who were the sole survivors. Happily, many of the officers and men posted as missing on the evening of this day were taken prisoners of war and it has been possible since to get from some of them their account of this day's fighting. In most cases though, their impressions, owing to the impossibility of knowing anything beyond their own immediate locality, added to the low-lying mist that hid everything more than 30 yards away, and the efflux of time, are not so complete as could be desired.

The preliminary bombardment lasted about four hours. " A " and " B " Companies in Noreuil Switch and Sidney Avenue suffered considerable casualties from the weight and accuracy of the barrage. The crash of enemy artillery was tremendous ; a sudden change from apparent inability to return our fire to a tornado of metal of all calibre. It is said that on the Bullecourt front alone the Germans used batteries whose guns ran well into four figures.

Day broke, but with its coming, visibility was little improved. A low clinging ground-mist enveloped the scene. Mist and the acrid vapour and smoke from bursting projectiles rendered near objects hazy and made those more than thirty or forty yards away invisible.

Back areas, too, came in for attention. Captain Clifford arrived at Achiet-le-Grand on his way back from leave late on the 20th and spent the night in the Church Hut there. Between 3 and 4 o'clock the next morning the Germans began to shell the place, landing them at the rate of one every three minutes. Leaving Achiet at eight he proceeded *via* Gomiecourt and Ervillers to our transport lines at Mory. All the way up he found the country systematically and generously treated by the German gunners.

All realized that the threatened offensive had begun, but Rear Headquarters could do nothing. The Quartermaster and Transport Officer went quietly on preparing the rations which they would take up that evening. At about 11.15 parties of men could be seen making their way back from the direction of L'Homme Mort, but they were only working-parties on their way back to billets, and had little news to tell.

Meanwhile the following message arrived by runner:

> Sent off at 7.5 a.m. From 2/5th Sherwood Foresters. In communication with both front battalions who report shelling general, but not very heavy a.a.a. All battalions are being gassed a.a.a. Greater part of shelling going west of Noreuil-Longatte road a.a.a. No sign of hostile attack as yet a.a.a.

Later, another runner arrived with a further message timed 8.30 a.m.:

> Hostile shelling still heavy, but gassing has ceased a.a.a. Casualties do not appear to be heavy but this is uncertain a.a.a.

Lieutenant Williamson, Brigade-Battalion Liaison Officer, went forward and sent back a runner with the information, timed 9.45 a.m.:

> Heavy shelling of front line 2nd system apparently from Quéant and Hendecourt a.a.a. Noreuil Valley heavily shelled a.a.a. No aeroplane activity and no machine-gun fire. So far as can be ascertained the enemy barrage has not yet lifted from the front line.

Another message from Colonel Gadd sent by runner at 10.40 a.m. stated:

> Enemy reported to be about C.11. a. 1.5. Enemy barrage on Pontefract and Dewesbury Trenches and enemy advancing a.a.a. Enemy also attacking near junction of Ilkney Support and Halifax a.a.a. Further unconfirmed reports state : Enemy have penetrated Dewesbury a.a.a. Am manning Noreuil-Longatte road and ready to form defensive flanks to right.

The last message to get through was sent off by Battalion Headquarters at 12 noon and read:

> Situation as follows. We are holding Noreuil Switch from C.9. d. 9.4. and road near Battalion Headquarters. Enemy have captured Dewesbury and Pontefract and appear to be digging in a.a.a. Have formed defensive flank down Noreuil Switch from C.9. d. 9.4 westwards. Enemy moving in large numbers along ridge C.17. c. a.a.a. Am prolonging my line along road towards Longatte a.a.a. Forces at my disposal estimated at 150 a.a.a.

After this, silence . . .

No further messages got through, and the story of what followed has to be pieced together from the evidence of many.

Lieutenant Williamson returned to Brigade Headquarters at 1 p.m. and reported that at 10.45 when nearing Battalion Headquarters enemy creeping barrage lifted on to the Noreuil-Longatte road. He remained at Headquarters for over an hour and returned to Noreuil village and valley, at which time the enemy were already in the village.

At about noon the Battalion rear-headquarters sent up runners to try and get into touch with companies. These returned during the afternoon with the information that they had not been allowed to proceed further than the third battle line and that the Germans were between that and Battalion Headquarters. This confirmed the rumour, already current, that the Battalion had been overwhelmed.

It must be remembered that the front line was being held by the 7th Sherwoods and the 2/5th were in support 600 to 1,000 yards behind. The rôle of the 2/5th was to attack across the open in the event of the enemy penetrating the front line. In this case the brigade in reserve would come up and take over the 2/5th positions, and no attempt to regain the lost ground was to be embarked upon until fresh troops came up.

A few days previously prisoners had been taken on the Corps front who stated that the enemy intended to attack on either the 20th or 21st and would use gas-shells during the preliminary bombardment.

This statement was remembered by at least one regimental officer when he found himself getting into his gas-mask on the morning of the 21st.

As the bombardment continued, casualties became more frequent. The Germans had many of our positions taped to a nicety. Pontefract Trench was a deep and well-dug trench, consequently " D " Company's casualties, though heavy, were nearly all head and neck wounds.

Looking out from this trench across the shallow valley, occasional glimpses were caught of forms, vague and shadowy, moving forward through the mist and smoke. It was the enemy in mass formation approaching our almost obliterated front line. The S.O.S. was sent up but was not responded to. It was probably never seen by our waiting gunners. Slowly the minutes passed to the men crouching in support. At about 11 the attack fell suddenly through the mist on " A " Company in Sidney Avenue. With great gallantry both " A " and " B " (adjoining in Noreuil Switch), opened rapid fire with rifles and Lewis-guns. The Germans were almost shoulder to shoulder ; it was impossible to miss them, and heavy losses were inflicted. But as soon as one wave went down before our fire others pressed in from behind and by sheer weight of numbers the garrison was overwhelmed.

Once in Sidney Avenue the Germans worked down it towards Pontefract. By this time Ecoust on the right, and Noreuil on the left of the Battalion's position, had given, and the enemy bringing up machine-guns were enfilading from the flanks, rendering the Ecoust and Noreuil road untenable. No direct attack was made on Pontefract Trench. The field-greys worked down it in large parties bombing our men out of it inch by inch. Above, a hail of machine-gun bullets traversed, swishing and cutting the air into strips, making it impossible for either " D " or " C " Company to counter-attack from above.

Meanwhile Battalion Headquarters had realized the position and Major Trench, the second-in-command, led a heroic but forlorn attempt down Sidney Avenue in an effort to stop the rush. Major Trench was hit three times, but stuck to it, and was eventually killed with many another gallant lad fighting with his back to the wall.

It is invidious to extol where all men were great, but Major Trench, though not a soldier by profession, had all those qualities that go to the making of a good officer.

He was not a comfortable man with whom to share a small dug-out. His personality was too big : his vitality and enthusiasm for work filled the atmosphere. He had enormous gifts for organization and great administrative ability. As second-in-command he had the oversight of the feeding and quartering arrangements of the Unit and it could not have been in better hands. He was to be found at all hours visiting the lines, the cook-house, helping to invent fresh dishes out of old material, altering and improving as new ideas came. Were the Battalion out at rest he would be off on his horse to replenish the canteen or to purchase vegetables as an extra for the men out of canteen funds. His especial pride were the field-kitchens. Woe to the senior cook whose brass work was not brightly polished, or whose dixies showed the slightest trace of grease. He instituted overalls to enable the cooks to keep themselves a little cleaner. He had bowls of disinfectant provided, into which the cooks could dip their hands before touching the food. On one occasion a staff officer came round inspecting and, pointing to one of the bowls, said "What's that? Eye-wash, I suppose." " No, sir," replied the nervous cook, " that's to dip our hands in."

Major Trench had spent the earlier period of the war training cadets with the Inns of Court. Feeling that he himself should share the hazard of the life for which he helped to train others he later transferred to the 2/5th. He was always ready to help and encourage young officers who came to the Battalion, and especially had a warm corner for any who had served in the Inns of Court. With all his practicability he had a mystic strain in him, probably due to his Irish origin. He was a great admirer of Donald Hankey and the latter's writings were his constant companion. Among all the splendid men that the Battalion lost on this tragic day, Trench was by no means the least.

To return. The visibility had by this time somewhat increased and low-flying 'planes came over in search of information. One of these saw that the attack was being held up by " C " Company's resistance round the sunken road and soon 5.9s were falling thickly, turning its vicinity into a human slaughterhouse.

The Lincolns and Leicesters, the Brigade in reserve, had now come up and were holding a trench about 400 yards in rear of Battalion Headquarters. Some of them had reached the Noreuil Switch, a trench on the north side and parallel to the valley, but they had been driven out of this.

Battalion Headquarters and the remnants of " C " Company were now surrounded and the survivors taken prisoners.

It is impossible, even if it were the business of the present historian, to criticize the Battalion for its failure to hold the enemy on this day. What blame there was, if any, must be left to others, with greater knowledge, thinking in armies and army corps, over wide defensive zones, to properly apportion.

Taking the one small corner in which our Battalion played out its part in the drama, it is certain that Colonel Gadd was not altogether satisfied with the relative dispositions of troops holding it. For among the papers issued a little earlier and which survived this day (Orders No. 69) we find the following, dated 20th, dealing with the reconnoitring of this sector by company commanders of the 2/5th :

(4) The Commanding Officer thinks that the present front line is held too strongly and the support line too weakly. Reconnaissance should determine the views of the company commanders concerned on this subject.

It is, however, doubtful, supposing the forward positions had been held weakly and the defence concentrated in depth, whether the results would have been different. Both the 7th and the 2/5th fought with the utmost vigour and gallantry against an enormous weight of men and metal.

One little corporal of " B " Company, when told by Mr. Sutherland, his Platoon Commander, that as far as he could see they were surrounded and there was not

much hope, turned to the men around him and said,
" Now, lads, remember you are British and fight—fight
for England!" Shortly afterwards he was killed. An
endeavour has been made to trace this lad's name, but
so far without success. It is deeds like this that should
make Nottinghamshire and Derbyshire proud of the
gallant boys she bred, lads who went willingly (though
not gladly) to the shambles for their country's sake.

It took the Germans eight hours to advance 2,000
yards. As Sir Douglas Haig says in his despatch : " At
the end of the first day, therefore, the enemy had made
very considerable progress, but he was still firmly held
in the battle zone, in which it had been anticipated that
the real struggle would take place. Nowhere had he
effected that immediate break through for which his
troops had been training for many weeks, and such progress as he had made had been bought at a cost which
has already reduced his chances of carrying out his ultimate purpose."

The enemy losses had been tremendous, but to the
Sherwood Brigade they had been, unfortunately, equally
heavy.

On the morning of the attack the 2/5th had in the line
30 officers and 614 other ranks. Out of this total of 644,
only 4 men reported back unwounded.

The losses among the officers were particularly heavy.
" A " Company had 1 killed and 2 wounded (out of 4),
" B " Company 3 killed and 3 wounded (out of 6). Major
Trench was also killed and Captain Judd, the Padre, was
wounded and afterwards died of wounds in German
hands. Of the six hundred men it is estimated that
about 180 must have been killed outright and over 200
wounded, many of them seriously ; the remaining 200
odd were taken prisoners.

From subsequent accounts the Germans do not appear
to have treated our men brutally, when captured.
Prisoners had the direction pointed out to them and had
to help carry back the wounded. Eventually they were
concentrated into groups and marched under escort to

the cage about 15 miles in rear. Most of them had had nothing to eat all day and were thoroughly exhausted when they reached it. Here black bread and weak coffee were given them.

The remnant of the Battalion at Mory now came under the command of Captain Clifford as senior serving officer. He was instructed by the Brigade to act on orders he would receive direct from Division.

The same afternoon they moved back to Courcelles, part of the transport remaining behind to take up ammunition if necessary. The night was spent there in an open field.

At 11 a.m. next day orders came to move and get back to Ayette, near Ablainzelle. The wagons had meanwhile gone back to Mory to fetch more stores. The Quartermaster who went back with them visited Brigade and received orders for every officer and man to go up at once. Captain Quibell had joined that morning from the 2/8th, and three officers and twenty-five other ranks, including the band, went up into the line on the right of Mory as a composite company under him, reporting at Behagnies at 6 p.m.

Contrary to expectation, they had a quiet time, and on the night of the 23rd were relieved and joined the remainder of the Brigade at Senlis. The transport had moved there earlier in the day. There a draft of 23 men practically doubled the strength of the Unit. On the 24th further reinforcements and the survivors joined.

Starting in the early hours (3 a.m.) of the following morning, the Battalion trekked 12 miles to Bavelincourt, passing on the way many refugees who were being evacuated from the villages as the Germans advanced. That night all had sumptuous billets in the Château. The next day a further march of 16 miles brought them to Fieffes, just south of Candas. Here 2nd Lieutenants Palmer and Cooke and about 23 men were picked up.

On the 28th transport and men proceeded by train to Laboissière and from there went by bus to Cambligneul.

March had opened with an effective strength of 48

officers and 950 other ranks. It closed with a ration strength of 6 officers and 204 other ranks.

During the morning of the last day of the month, His Majesty King George paid the Battalion a visit. He inspected the men quite informally and chatted to them in a friendly way. His unceremonious manner and obvious deep concern for the fate of the men left at Bullecourt did much to hearten the remnant.

The same afternoon the G.O.C. 59th Division came and also inspected the residue.

CHAPTER IX

MOUNT KEMMEL

" For after all there are only two nations, France and England,
the rest are nothing." (A saying of Napoleon.)
—LORD ROSEBERY : *The Last Phase.*

FROM Cambligneul on April 1st, the Battalion entrained
at Aubigny for Proven. From here the men footed it
five miles to Roads Camp at St. Jahn-ter-Biezen, the
transport meanwhile covering the whole distance by
road.

The next few days were spent in reorganization.
Major R. S. Pratt, M.C., rejoined from another Sherwood
battalion and took over command, being posted as second
in command. A new Medical Officer arrived to take the
place of Capt. Mearns, 2nd Lieut. M. D. Barrows became
Adjutant and Captain C. N. Littleboy, M.C., who had
been on Brigade Headquarters for some little while,
returned and took over his old company.

At the same time reinforcements were rushed up from
the Infantry Base Depôt at Calais at a rapid rate and
began to pour in. In the first days of the month drafts
amounting to about 400 men put in an appearance, some
of them arriving in the middle of the night, after several
days spent in tracking the Unit down from one resting
place to another.

At 3 p.m. on the 3rd, General Plumer, commanding
the 2nd Army, inspected the Battalion and gave the
officers a short talk on the general situation.

There was plenty of work to be done. Men had to be
posted to companies ; Lewis-guns had to be tested and
fired ; short kits had to be checked and put in order ;
N.C.Os. had to be promoted. Luckily some of the best
N.C.Os. had been on leave, or away on courses, during

the operations culminating in the tragedy of March 21st.
These now returned and formed the framework around
which the new Battalion was to grow and become the
2/5th with the 2/5th tradition. The officers with the
Battalion at this juncture were, Major Pratt, Captains
Clifford, Quibell and Littleboy, 2nd Lieutenants Ford,
Jacques, Palmer, Cooke and Barrows, Lieutenant
Farnsworth (Quartermaster), Lieutenant Spendlove
(Transport Officer), and the Medical Officer, Lieutenant
Cossar.

On the 7th the Battalion marched to Winnezeele and
were billeted in scattered farms. From there, three days
later, the men were entrained late in the afternoon and
proceeded by light railway to the Cheese Market, Poperinghe. Detraining, the companies were marched via
Switch road and the Ypres-Poperinghe road to St.
Laurence Camp, Brandhoek.

These roads were old acquaintances to some few of
the officers and men. But to the reinforcements, boys of
19 just out, the route recalled no memories. It was
perhaps as well this march was taken after dark. The
Germans had shelled the area heavily, and disembowelled
horses, and other things beside the road, were no sight for
lads new to the glories of war.

On the 12th the new Commanding Officer arrived,
Major (now Lieut.-Colonel) J. C. Baines (Leicestershire
Regiment), and, almost simultaneously, orders came to
move. This gave Colonel Baines little immediate
chance of getting to know his men, but those were the
days of the German Push, and events moved rapidly.

The Battalion went by Decauville to La Clytte, detrained and marched towards Kemmel. The Colonel
had been previously ordered to meet the Brigadier on
the road north of Kemmel village and rode off leaving
the Battalion to follow. The Brigadier, General Stansfeld,
C.M.G., D.S.O., had no orders, and said that very little
was known of the general situation except that the enemy
had broken our line and had captured the Messines Ridge.
The G.S.O. 2, 19th Division, to which the 178th Brigade

had been lent, joined the party, pointed out Wytschaete, and told the C.O. that the 2/5th might have to relieve the remnant of the South African Infantry Brigade who were holding that village.

The Battalion, in the meanwhile, had halted by the roadside further back. The only thing to do was to clear the road and wait. The field-kitchens which had gone on to Locre were sent for, and a hot meal prepared and eaten in the dark.

Although various vague orders arrived at intervals, none of them spelt move, and the Battalion bivouacked for the night in an open field off the Kemmel-La Clytte road. There was much to do. Rations had to be issued, and Lewis-guns overhauled. All this was carried on in heavy darkness livened by occasional bomb and shell burst which, however, caused no casualties. The transport, which had accompanied the Battalion, was sent back to Westoutre.

The officers managed after much scrounging to commandeer a camp warden's hut close by, and here—amongst a labyrinth of bowls, forms, palliasses and other odds and ends of camp stores—long and serious discussions were held settling details regarding possible action. Colonel Baines showed himself a pastmaster in the art of administration, and it was largely owing to his preliminary settlement of important details that the Battalion during the ensuing week brought such great credit to the Regiment.

Breakfast the next morning was fixed for a very early hour, it being thought better to have it at 6 a.m. than to run the risk of having none at all.

This proved a wise precaution, for at 7.30 a.m. orders came to move forward to fill a gap in the line between T.11 Central and T.10. a. on the Neuve Eglise-Wulverghem road, and to be ready to attack if called upon to do so.

The Battalion moved at 7.45 a.m., the Commanding Officer going on to get further particulars from the Brigadier. Halting at the Lindenhoek Cross-roads all officers met, maps were produced and orders issued,

whilst outside the carpenter's shop, in which the council
was held, shells hurtled and crashed in a manner calculated to disturb the nerves of the most phlegmatic.

It is perhaps as well to give here, before going deeper
into the story of the operations and movements that
followed, some indication of the make-up of the Unit
as it stood that day at company interval on the road at
Lindenhoek.

The old 2/5th, made up of men with many months of
training and campaigning together, was gone. In its
place was a Battalion, much under strength, made up
chiefly of young boys of 19 and others, rushed out quickly
to fill the big gaps in fighting regiments. Very few of
them knew much about the Lewis-gun, and the Lewis-gun
was at this time our main weapon in defence. Most of
the men, too, were strangers to each other. Each company had been hastily organized, 130 men to a company,
and platoons formed. There was a shortage of N.C.Os.,
but what N.C.Os. there were took command of the platoons as there were no officers available.

The Commanding Officer, Lieut.-Colonel J. C. Baines,
had only joined the previous day, and had not had time
as yet to learn the names of his officers, though these were
so few in number as to be little more than one per company. Captain Quibell, D.S.O., was in command of " A,"
2nd Lieut E. E. Ford of " B," Captain Littleboy, M.C.,
was in charge of " C," and 2nd Lieut. J. N. Jacques,
assisted by 2nd Lieut. W. Cook, was in command of
" D " Company. Battalion Headquarters consisted of
the Colonel, Major Pratt, M.C. (2nd in command), 2nd
Lieut. M. D. Barrows (Adjutant), Lieut. E. H. G. Palmer
(Signalling Officer), Lieut. J. Farnsworth (Quartermaster),
Lieut. Spendlove (Transport Officer), and Lieut. G. C.
Cossar (Medical Officer). In addition, Captain Clifford
was retained at Headquarters in reserve and to assist,
but was very soon called upon for company work.

These, then, the officers, and these the material with
which they had to work, who now were ordered forward
to fill a gap reported just south of the Neuve Eglise-

Wulverghem road. How these raw boys of 19 answered the call made upon them it will now be my business to tell.

" A " and " C " Companies, under instructions, threw out an advance-guard and moved down the road to the railway crossing in the Douve valley, and then, pushing forward a covering screen, worked across country in artillery formation to the gap, with orders that if, when they arrived at their map co-ordinates, they found the Germans in possession, they were to attack and drive them out.

" B " and " D " followed in support, and came to rest at the railway, one company each side of the road. They were immediately ordered to dig, and very soon, owing to the close proximity of an R.E. dump, made themselves very comfortable indeed. B.H.Q. was established in a small dug-out under the railway.

Lieut. Palmer had meanwhile taken forward a patrol to glean information. The Headquarters of a Gloucester Battalion was passed, but they had no news as to what was happening ahead. The road had been badly smashed, but, luckily, things were, for the moment, quiet.

" A " and " C " Companies reached their positions at about 11 a.m. with few casualties, and found the 80th Field Company Royal Engineers lying there in shell-holes and ditches. These men had been pushed in there under the stress of events to partially fill the gap, and were very pleased to see our men arrive. They were, for the time being, incorporated with the 2/5th and came under Colonel Baines' command. On taking over, our fellows were warned by the R.E. Composite Company that some Germans were about masquerading in British uniforms, but the 2/5th did not see any. However, the Major of the R.Es. was challenged one night by the 7th Battalion (who were on the left of " C " Company), did not answer quickly enough, and was shot. He was a fine fellow, held the M.C. (and bar), and his death was one of those unfortunate and regrettable accidents often paralleled, but apparently unavoidable, in war.

In efforts to establish a line of posts along the road,
" A " and " C " met with hostile machine-gun fire from
the enemy, who held a ridge about 550 yards away slightly
north-east of Neuve Eglise. These companies quickly
got into touch with the regiments on either flank, but
found they were holding on with very few men. The
position on the right in particular, owing to lack of men,
was extremely precarious.

" C " Company in their love for pleasant scenery
placed their Headquarters in an orchard within easy
reach of a deserted Church Army hut, still containing,
at least until " C " Company got near it, cigarettes. For
it must be remembered that our men were now operating
over ground which, until a few days previously, had been
a back area covered with rest billets for English troops.

" A " Company Headquarters had coolly taken up
their official residence in a small house beside the road
actually *in front* of the front line. To reach it visitors
had to crawl along a muddy ditch and dash across a road
under observation from the enemy. His machine-guns
covering this approach were responsible for about ten
casualties that day. However, the Lewis-guns of " A "
and " C " were equally alert and more than equalized
matters. These 19-year-old boys took to the war game
like ducks to water, and, although they were raw and new,
and lying in mud with little cover, they were extraordinarily cheery and spirited. Later in the day very heavy
shelling from Messines Ridge, in enfilade and of large
calibre, took place. The two supporting companies and
Headquarters came in for most of it and suffered forty
casualties. Here again the young boys, whose first
experience this was of intensive shell-fire, behaved
splendidly.

At 4 p.m. the Battalion was ordered to extend the
right flank to relieve a company of Worcesters, and did
so, linking up with the Gloucesters.

The general situation now appeared to be that our
forces were holding the old trench line running west of
Sparbrokneolen to east of Wulverghem, thence, swinging

M

south-west, to Neuve Eglise, with a reserve line along the Kemmel-Neuve Eglise road. The position in Neuve Eglise and on the right flank was a little vague. The Gloucesters on the right of the 2/5th held the reserve line facing east, and their right ran at right angles into the front line held by our men.

The evening came on and nothing further happened, though an attack was expected any minute. As fighting had been going on in and around Neuve Eglise all the day, it was most difficult to obtain accurate information of the situation. Heavy indirect machine-gun fire did not tend to increase one's peace of mind ; it was realized only too well that the front line, consisting as it did of a few isolated posts, could not possibly hold up a heavy attack. Lieut. G. C. Cossar, the Medical Officer, did splendid work all night long. His Aid Post was in a cellar close to B.H.Q. and to this place a constant stream of wounded was always flowing.

The long night at last gave way to dawn, and so a day of great uneasiness arrived. At 7.30 a.m. shelling increased very considerably, and now became a hurricane bombardment of our support positions and all approaches around Kemmel.

Reports early on came in that Neuve Eglise had fallen, but, coming from stragglers, they could not be relied upon very much. Actually the enemy did get a foothold in this village during the morning, but was quickly driven out, and our positions there completely restored.

Soon after eleven o'clock, the enemy was reported massing opposite our own front, and harassing fire was at once opened by our artillery. A half-hearted attack was made at 1 p.m., but the rifles and Lewis-guns of " A " and " C " Companies quickly repulsed it, assisted by a company of the 2/6th Sherwoods, who came up to strengthen our right and the 7th who came in at the same time on our left. The enemy withdrew and appeared to be digging in along the Leeurk Farm Ridge.

Later in the afternoon Captain Quibell, D.S.O., O.C.

"A" Company, was wounded severely in the right leg, which had subsequently to be amputated ; C.S.M. Lees, temporarily assumed command. Soon afterwards 2nd Lieut. E. E. Ford was gassed, and so "A" and "B" Companies had not a single officer left. Captain H. M. Clifford from B.H.Q. then took over "B" Company.

The positions of "B" and "D" Companies became more and more untenable, owing to the sustained shelling, in which former British 8in. guns were taking a big share, and it was decided to sideslip them into a line of old trenches in T.3. d. 5.8, and T.4. d. 9.1, about 800 north and in rear of their present positions. This move was carried out just before dusk, and was evidently observed, for out in the open heavy shelling caught the rear of "D" Company, and six men were killed and fourteen wounded. Captain Clifford who had just taken over "B" Company was also wounded. At this juncture, luckily, two officers reported from the 7th Battalion, 2nd Lieut. Spatcher, who took command of "A" Company, and 2nd Lieut. Green, who took over "B" Company.

At 6 p.m. Neuve Eglise was again and finally captured by the enemy, but our front line still held on in position. "A" and "C" Companies were now in a very precarious situation. The enemy were through on the immediate right of "A" Company, and it was only a question of time before they became cut off.

Battalion Headquarters was now established at N.32. d. 7.9, and here at 11.30 p.m. the C.O. of the 2/6th Sherwoods brought orders that the front line companies were to withdraw through the support line to Kingsway Trench, T.4. a. 0.3, to T.5. a. 3.2. This movement was completed by 6 a.m., "A" Company passing through at 4.25 a.m. and "C" Company at 4.30 a.m.

"B" and "D" Companies thus became the new front line. This withdrawal proved a most difficult task, "A" and "C" Companies having to retreat across rough country covered with dykes and hedges, but everything passed off smoothly in spite of the pitch dark

night, and by 4.30 a.m. on the 15th the withdrawal had
been safely accomplished without loss.

During the night the new front line was hastily
organized for defence. The trenches were old and had
fallen in almost everywhere, and where they weren't knee-
deep in water they were lined with a deep carpet of mud.
" D " Company on the left were holding a front of 800
yards with a strength of seventy men, and further, on
their left, linked up with an Irish battalion just about
as happily situated.

As dawn approached another violent bombardment
began, this time from front, flank and rear. As suddenly
as it began it broke off, and the enemy could be seen
advancing in small parties with light machine-guns. The
attack was directed at " D " Company and from them
further to the left. For a minute the men of " D "
Company failed to realize the situation, but having done
so, they rose to the occasion splendidly, and soon rifles
and Lewis-guns were reaping a rich harvest. 2nd Lieut.
Jacques made his way along from post to post and was
glad to find the Irish, on his left, still in position. He
discovered an officer, but the latter could not say what
had happened further on, towards Wulverghem. However, this particular bit of front was maintained intact,
much to the relief of B.H.Q. who feared the worst.

The Germans, somewhat shaken at such an unexpec-
tedly nasty reception, withdrew to about 500 yards
distance, and things quietened down for a spell. " D "
Company's enthusiastic display of musketry had bluffed
them, and they made no attempt to push on, which was
lucky, for the few posts held by " D " Company would
certainly have been overwhelmed. But the enemy were
not quiet for long, and very soon machine-guns began
to make things very unpleasant. From this sniping
" D " Company had frequent casualties, unavoidable
owing to their exposed position. The left flank caused great
anxiety, for, if Wulverghem fell, it would then become
impossible to hold the present line. Touch with the
108th Brigade was never quite gained, and "A " Company

of the 7th Sherwoods moved up to fill the gap. Complete touch, however, was made with the 2/6th Sherwoods dug in north of the railway on our right. About 8.15 a.m. a telephone message was received at B.H.Q. stating that the 108th Brigade had been pushed in about N.29. central. "C" Company, now one of the supporting companies, immediately formed a defensive flank facing east. Thus the first intimation of the fall of Wulverghem came from B.H.Q. Late in the afternoon 2nd Lieut. Cook was sent to withdraw the men on the extreme left, and, if possible, to find out what had happened to the other unit. No trace of them was found, but it was obvious that Wulverghem was German, for enemy machine-guns were firing from that direction. Shelling became very violent, much of it from the direction of Messines, enfilading "D" Company completely. Two Lewis-guns were blown up and most of the gunners were casualties. The men still stuck it out splendidly, but were done to the wide : 2nd Lieut. Jacques made urgent representations for reinforcements. Two platoons from "A" Company were sent to support them, their arrival doing much to hearten the remnant of "D" Company, now about forty strong. This left only three platoons definitely in hand in support.

The enemy had a balloon up over Wulverghem way and had complete observation of any movement.

During the day men were seen working forward either to form a line or preparatory to an assault.

Lieutenant Palmer had a forward Headquarters at the head of buried cable near Daylight Corner, and rendered invaluable service in getting messages through quickly.

At 3 p.m. information was received from Brigade that the Irish Battalion reported the enemy to be in Elbow Farm, on "C" Company's left and "D" Company's rear. This message was passed on to O.C. "C" Company with instructions that ended with—" if occupied, turn the b——s out." Lance-Corporal Boyes, with two men of "C" Company, undertook to confirm this, but found the place unoccupied.

Night fell and the shelling lessened somewhat. It was decided to settle the left flank mystery at once. Lance-Corporal Thompson and three picked men patrolled beyond the last man of " D " Company, and a short way along the trench had a nasty shock. It was full of Germans, and it was hard to say which were most astonished. Pursued by wild erratic rifle-fire the patrol got away and hastened back to Company Headquarters. The situation was put before B.H.Q. at once, and in the meanwhile " D " Company held on. Towards midnight their position was in immediate danger of being quietly surrounded. The enemy were in front, on the immediate left, and were also working round behind them ; fortunately for our men much time was wasted, and no direct attack was attempted.

At 1 a.m. a very famous message arrived, and deserves to be reproduced in full. This was " Ax. 101," and was as follows :

> At 2 a.m. night 15-16th (to-night) the Battalion will withdraw from the present position under company arrangements aaa. Platoons should be collected, and moved together. " B " and " D " Companies will co-operate in this move and " A " and " C " Companies. " B," " D " and " C " Companies will have a small outpost screen out in present line until 2.45 a.m. which will then be withdrawn.
>
> Route : Lindenhoek Cross-roads—Kemmel-Locre road.
>
> Control and guide posts are established at Cross-road N.21. d. 4.3—Fork-roads, N.21. c. 9.6 and Cross-roads N.19. c. 8.0.
>
> On reaching area N.25. b. (i.e., behind Kemmel Hill), companies will re-organize and remain in platoon groups and report location to B.H.Q. at N.25. b. 9.1 (Kemmel Dug-out).
>
> A Battalion guide will be at N.19. c. 8.0 to show company runners way to Battalion Headquarters.
>
> O.C. companies will take out with them any platoons temporarily attached to them.
>
> Distribute and take out any S.A.A. Lewis-guns, drums, etc. in hand.
>
> Report centre at Test Point, will close at 2 a.m.
>
>> Present B.H.Q., closed 3 a.m.
>> New   ,,   opens 2.30 a.m.
>> R.A.P. at new B.H.Q.
>> Acknowledge.

The evacuation was a much more difficult operation than would appear on paper, especially in the case of " D " Company holding a big frontage. It was a dark night, raining slightly and inclined to be misty. Sergeant F. E. Handley had a large share in " D " Company's successful withdrawal, the prompt way in which he collected each post and closed them on to the right made the rest of the task quite easy. " D " Company got away in three parties and arranged to unite in Kemmel. 2nd Lieut. Cook took the first, Sergeant Handley the second, and the remainder under 2nd Lieut. Jacques followed about half an hour later. Throughout the withdrawal shelling was very slight, and the Germans were evidently unaware of what was toward. The Battalion arrangements for guides worked splendidly, and by 5 a.m. the 2/5th was reunited. A dense mist had risen by now, and the guide who should have directed the company commanders to the new B.H.Q. was not in evidence. These unfortunates then set out in search of the place, and after a weary tramp all over Kemmel Hill ultimately discovered it.

Visions of a long peaceful sleep came before the eyes of the company commanders on learning from the C.O. that the Battalion was now in reserve. With lighter hearts they made their way back to their respective companies, and proceeded to billet them in the various hutted camps scattered about. Hardly was this done and parties sent to B.H.Q. for rations, when 8 in. shells began to fall. Each company commander then acted in the only way possible, if the Germans wanted the huts for targets they could have them. " A " Company found an old concrete hut, ankle deep in water, but, scrounging duckboards, they made the place tolerably comfortable, and were, if somewhat crowded, at least fairly safe. " C " Company and " B " dropped on farms which seemed out of the prevailing storm of crumps. " D " Company were scattered in various old bivouacs dug into a steep bank, and some were placed in a French Aid Post, a dug-out on the roadside. Meanwhile " D "

Company's ration party under Mr. Cook had met with heavy shelling and had stayed in the cellar of a farm. . . . A few minutes later a shell smashed this place, and Mr. Cook was terribly wounded. Six of the men carried him as far as the Convent at Locre, where he died a few hours later. His loss cast a gloom over " D " Company with whom he was extremely popular. Neither very big nor very old, he was just one of the many " Second Lieutenants unless otherwise stated " who did their job well and conscientiously, and crowded the casualty lists day by day as they passed westward.

During the day no movement of companies was called for, and the men got a certain amount of rest. The officers, of necessity, had constantly to go to Battalion Headquarters and run the gauntlet of the still violent shelling.

The scene at B.H.Q. baffles all description. All sorts of headquarters were in the tunnel, and though it could not be damaged by shell-fire, German artillery concentrated continually on all approaches to it. Outside, dead lay everywhere, many killed whilst carrying messages, others hit at the entrances to the tunnel. Brushwood, uprooted trees, smashed-up transport limbers and guns added to the general scene of destruction. Kemmel Hill, which in 1915 was one of the quietest parts of the British front, was now little more than an open-air mortuary.

Later at night five officers of the West Yorkshire Regiment arrived, a very welcome sight for the four company commanders who had spent several days and nights without sleep.

The 17th arrived and with it the French. Our officers knew they were coming, but none of the men knew, and the latter first looked amazed and then extremely happy when, as dawn broke, the famous French 75s roared out a greeting to the enemy. They had moved into position during the night and seemed to be everywhere ; a wonderful tonic to troops fed to the teeth.

It was a day of further trials, of gap-filling and trench

digging, and, as is usually the case, nothing to show for
it all. The enemy were repeatedly attacking, and companies had to make frequent moves as the situation required. They all had more or less similar experiences,
so it will suffice to describe the wanderings of " D " on
this particular day. Beginning in the bivouacs dug in a
bank off the Kemmel-Locre road, shelling grew so bad
that these positions became untenable, chiefly through a
heavy concentration of gas. A move was made to the
farm where " C " Company had spent most of the previous
day. Here " D " Company settled down for a few hours'
rest. However, early in the afternoon they were ordered
to move forward into a trench close to Battalion Headquarters, and this move was carried out without loss.
Soon after five o'clock, " A " Company were put in the
line to hold a reported gap, and " D " Company moved
over the hill to the forward slope, and took over " A "
Company's position in some badly-battered trenches.
At 2 a.m. the French took over from " A " Company, and
the latter were ordered to withdraw to their previous
position, and " D " back to the reverse slope of the Hill.

The lack of platoon officers and senior N.C.Os. rendered all these moves extremely difficult to carry out ;
the prospect of a heavy shell amongst the company
whilst in the open was unpleasant to dwell upon.

In the meantime the reasons for these quick changes
and moves were not far to seek. The Germans were
pressing their attacks, our line was weakly held, and the
position at various points vague and continually shifting.
All wires were cut to Brigade quite early on the 17th.
A message arrived stating that both flanks of the 7th
Sherwoods had been penetrated, and a Lancashire Fusilier
officer came in with the report of a heavy attack on the
right and asked for reinforcements. All through the day
rumours and reports of attacks came in and the position
of the right flank beyond the Lancashire Fusiliers (held
by oddments, apparently a few West Yorks. made up
with the VIII Corps Schools) was obscure. Gaps, too,
were continually reported and had to be covered. The

situation was so vague that it was difficult to judge as to
the correctness of the reports. However, the left seemed
safe ; it was on the right flank, which embraced the re-
entering valleys of the south-west slopes of Kemmel Hill,
that the danger spot appeared to lie.

" A " Company therefore moved up to counter-attack
if required, with " D " Company in support. " B "
formed a defensive flank and " C " Company held a
watching brief in close reserve.

An officer patrol under Lieutenant Palmer was sent
out and gained touch with the 1st Leicesters at N.31. a.
0.5, and found that Battalion very uneasy as to the
position on the right.

Meanwhile, at 3.15 p.m. this afternoon (17th), the 99th
Infantry Regiment 28th Division French Army arrived
on the scene. At this time the shelling was terrific and
one battalion of this Regiment was so badly cut up by it
that it had to be sent back and its place taken by a fresh
battalion.

Once again, at 4.45 p.m., a gap was reported in the
front line, from N.31. a. 0.5 to N.31. b. 0.5. " A " Company filled this, the other companies taking part in the
general post.

Later in the day the French took over this gap and
" A " Company and the others echeloned backwards, to
their previous positions.

The same afternoon officers from the 177th Infantry
Brigade came up to study the situation.

The night wore on, upon the whole, quietly.

Suddenly, at 4.30 a.m. on the 18th, an intense hurricane
bombardment of 5.9s, heavy 8-inch and lighter whizz-
bangs broke over and about Kemmel Hill. The air was
cut and rent into slithers by the swift passage of projectiles. The earth was ground into fine powder ; tree
roots and camp debris was spouted and vomited sky-
wards as the guns thundered and crashed. " A "
Company, crouching in the battered trenches on the sum-
mit of the hill (which they had reoccupied on their relief
by the French), caught the full force of this mighty

barrage. Their plight beggars description. One particular corner crowded with men had been blown to
pieces, six men had completely disappeared   . fragments of bodies lay about.

The 9th Royal Irish Rifles came up to help beat off the
threatened attack, and were placed near the Windmill.
They lost 100 men through shell-fire before they reached
our positions.

At about 11 o'clock the attack developed. The
Lancashire Fusiliers reported strong enemy attack from
Donegal Farm. Earlier in the morning the French had
penetrated this farm and had killed or taken prisoner
the whole of its garrison. Now the S.O.S. was sent back
by carrier pigeons and our artillery behind quickly put
down their counter-barrage. Under it the German
advance withered and broke.

Soon after this " A " and " D " Companies were
pushed on to the forward slope of the hill, in readiness for
counter-attack purposes. Os.C. " A " and " D " Companies made a personal reconnaissance of the ground
where trouble was expected, and at once sent in a joint
report that there was no sign of enemy activity. The
same runner brought back an order for an immediate
counter-attack! The French G.O.C. had asked for this,
having been informed that his line west of Donegal
Farm had been pierced. Os.C. " A " and " D " knew
very well that up to ten minutes previously there had
been nothing doing, but orders were orders, and so,
marshalling their respective forces, they moved forward
to counter-attack. *En route* they had a pretty rough
time, but managed to reach the French support line
without loss. This was a sunken road, and just as they
got there, a perspiring runner caught them up with
orders not to counter-attack, but to hold support
trenches. These, needless to say, wanted digging, but the
soil was soft and each company took over a piece of the
road and proceeded to dig in. In about an hour they
had got fine cover and the few casualties suffered were
mostly by men moving about. Shelling was periodically

very violent, but did no damage. It was not so nice about 5 o'clock, when for some unknown reason the French 75s dropped a most excellent barrage on that road, and for five minutes there was a wonderful mixture of French and British swear words!!

The explanation of this barrage, it was later discovered, was that it had been put down in response to a report that the enemy were again massing for an attack.

Late that night a message arrived with the glad tidings that, on receipt of the code letters " O.K.," the 2/5th would be relieved by the French. Hundreds of Frenchmen arrived at midnight and crowded that sunken road, but no " O.K. " message came, and the place began to resemble the main approach to a football ground on a Saturday afternoon.

The hours passed slowly ; the night turned very cold and snow began to fall thickly. The relief was slow and troublesome, owing to the difficulty of making the French understand the situation. Finally just as daylight broke the Battalion got away, marched back and concentrated at a farm just north of Westoutre where the first line transport had been located.

The total casualties during this period were : killed, 1 officer 32 other ranks : died of wounds, 3 other ranks ; wounded, 3 officers 135 other ranks ; missing, 30 other ranks. Total 204.

As a testimony to the severity of the fighting the following note from the 19th Divisional and 9th Corps Commanders is given :

Headquarters, IX. Corps G.

I wish to place on record my appreciation of the good work of the 178th Infantry Brigade whilst it was attached to 19th Division during the recent operations between April 12th and 19th. This Brigade under Brigadier General T. W. Stansfeld, D.S.O., maintained its position in front of Kemmel Hill with the utmost steadiness and gallantry, and I request that my thanks and appreciation of its service be conveyed to the G.O.C. 59th Division.

(Sgd.) G. D. JEFFREY, Major-General

19th Division,   Commanding 19th Division.
23rd April, 1918.

VIII Corps. Forwarded.

I hope you will also convey to the 178th Brigade my recognition and admiration of the fighting qualities shown in the very efficient assistance they afforded to 9th Troops in the serious engagement in which they recently took part.

(Sgd.) A. H. GORDON, Lieut.-General,
Commanding IX Corps.

24/4/18.

The following letter written by the Commanding Officer to the Derbyshire Territorial Association speaks for itself :

B.E.F. 6/7/18.

Dear Sir.

I think it due to the town of Derby that some record should be sent to your Association of the gallant deeds of one of its Territorial Battalions.   The Battalion in question, the 2/5th Battalion Sherwood Foresters, whom I have the honour to command, was engaged in operations from April 12th to 19th during the second big hostile offensive this year.   The Battalion went into action in the country round ———, and for seven days and nights without respite, under the most trying conditions possible, maintained their positions, only retiring when definitely ordered to do so.   In spite of heavy losses and continuous shelling of a most trying description the men were steady, beat off every hostile attack and responded to all calls made on their courage and endurance.

The operations were intricate and the country difficult, but the able leading of the Company Commanders enabled all things to be surmounted triumphantly, and the Battalion earned the thanks and praise of the Division to which we were temporarily attached.   I never wish to command a finer set of officers and men, and was proud to be associated with the Battalion in what was, I believe, their crowning achievement.   As some proof of what I say I give you a list of immediate awards won during this engagement, the large number of which gained in a week's fight is most unusual, and is a performance of which any Battalion in the Service may well be proud.

Distinguished Service Order : Lieut.-Col. J. C. Baines, 4th Leicester Regt. att. 2/5th Sherwood Foresters.   Military Cross : T/Lieut. G. C. Cossar, R.A.M.C. att. 2/5th Sherwood Foresters, Lieut. M. B. Drysdale, 2/5th Sherwood Foresters, 2/Lieut. N. F. Spatcher 7th., att. 2/5th Sherwood Foresters, A/Captain J. N. Jacques, 2/5th Sherwood Foresters.   Distinguished Conduct Medal : Sergeant R. F. Ford, M.M. Military medal : Sergeant F. E. Handley, Sergeant L. Garton, Sergeant (A/C.S.M.) P. Pearson, Corporal H.

Holmes, Corporal H. Jebb, Corporal H. Mosby, L/Corporal
W. Marshall, Ptes. T. Andrews, T. Charnley, A. Peterson,
A. H. Cragg, W. R. Whittaker, H. Hardcastle, A. Colledge,
A. Ford, T. Macpherson, A. Demain, all of the 2/5th Notts
and Derby Regiment.

I hope you will communicate to your Association my appreciation of the gallantry and devotion of all ranks.

Yours truly,

J. C. BAINES, Lieut.-Col.

Commanding 2/5th Sherwood Foresters.

To the Secretary,
Territorial Force Association for the County of Derby.

Sir Douglas Haig also paid tribute to the splendid
stand made by the English troops at Kemmel Hill
during this trying period.   He says :

" These attacks (i.e., on Meteren-Wytschaete) were
followed on the morning of the 17th April by a determined attempt on the part of the enemy to capture the
commanding feature known as Kemmel Hill.   The
assault was launched after a preliminary bombardment
of great intensity, and was accompanied by strong attacks
in the Meteren and Menis sectors.

" The enemy's attacks in the Kemmel sector were
pressed with great determination; but ended in his
complete repulse at all points by troops of the 34th, 49th,
and 19th Divisions,* his infantry being driven out by
counter-attacks, wherever they had obtained a temporary footing in our line."

* It must not be forgotten that the 178th Brigade was attached
to the 19th Division.   Kemmel Hill and village were not captured
till 10 a.m. on 25th April.

CHAPTER X

THE ARRIVAL OF THE AMERICANS

" This will have the happiest effect on my people." General Lee's remark to General Grant after surrender at the close of the American Civil War.

AT 8 a.m. on the 20th April the Battalion entrained, as it had so often done before, and went by Decauville from Heksen to Dirty Bucket Camp north of Brandhoek. The camp was a poor one and well deserved its name. But nobody minded how muddy and rotten the camp was. It was sufficient to know that the Battalion was *en route* for the back areas and that the Devil's cauldron, boiling and spouting around Kemmel, had been left behind, it was hoped, for ever.

However, only one day was spent at Dirty Bucket, and the men employed their time shaking themselves free from the slime and dirt they had accumulated during the previous week's fighting.

The evening of the 21st saw the Battalion in Shrine Camp, Houtkerque, after a ten miles' march. The next four days passed peacefully enough. Rest and a little training was the order of the day, though one day was given to helping to dig the Watou-Caestre defensive trench line. A draft of 12 officers and 81 other ranks arrived and helped somewhat to make the 2/5th feel more like a Battalion and less like a stray platoon.

Suddenly on the 26th, in the very middle of a football match, orders came and by 5.30 p.m. packing was finished and the Battalion was *en route* for St. Jahn-ter-Biezen as Divisional reserve. Here in Roads Camp the 2/5th stood-to, ready to move at an hour's notice, all that night and the next day *and* the day after that. Once orders did arrive to move, only to be cancelled fifteen minutes later.

On the 29th the threatened danger, whatever it may have been, had apparently been averted, for the Battalion on this day were allowed to move back again to Houtkerque. Here it was under canvas, which was not so pleasant as it might have been, owing to the dull cold weather. In the two days the Unit remained here the Lewis-gunners got one day's practice on the range, and eight picked shots (snipers) per company also got some target practice. Football, of course, occupied the afternoons.

On the 2nd, another dull day, in accordance with orders the Battalion marched to K.17. a. (which happened to be a field near Watou) to dig a line of trenches from Watou to Abeele. " A " Company moved off at 10 a.m. to pitch tents, the remainder, less the quartermaster stores and the bulk of the transport, which did not move, following in the early afternoon.

Late on the night of the fourth the Adjutant was awakened and told to be ready to move. Very heavy firing had been going on along the front that day and the worst was feared. But the general wind-up quickly gave place to curiosity when it became known that St. Omer was the destination.

At 7.50 a.m. on the 5th May the Battalion marched out about two miles towards Watou; from there it proceeded by bus to St. Omer, where it was billeted in the French barracks.

The next morning the reason for this sudden descent upon St. Omer became generally known. The Battalion was to be broken up. And not only the Battalion, the whole of the 59th Division was about to be disbanded. It was a great blow to all. All ranks felt that if they must soldier they would rather soldier with the Unit they had learned to love. But there was no hope. The enormous drain of the past months' fighting upon the reinforcement depôts had convinced General Headquarters that, in order to keep first-line divisions up to strength, others must go. The 59th Division was among these latter unfortunates. As Haig's official dispatch puts it :

The immense weight of the enemy's first and heaviest onslaughts in March and April, and the unprecedented masses of men and material employed by him, had called for practically the whole strength of the British Armies to withstand them, and had left our forces greatly weakened. Although prompt steps had been taken by the home authorities to dispatch to France as rapidly as possible all reinforcements then available in England, as well as to recall considerable bodies of troops from other theatres of war, these reinforcements required time to arr ve. . . .

Meanwhile it had become possible to maintain at an effective strength the full nu ber of our Divisions. At the beginning of May no less than eight Divisions (the 14th, 16th, 31st, 34th, 39th, 40th, 59th, 66th) had been reduced to cadres and were temporarily written off altogether as fighting units.

The whole day was spent in preparing rolls, checking kits, and cleaning up. Both the Brigadier and the G.O.C. 59th Division came and said farewell to the men drawn up in the barrack square.

At tea-time on the 7th, 15 officers and 560 other ranks marched to the station and entrained for the I.B.D. at Calais. There, the officers and men who had stood together during the terrible week round Kemmel were split up and drafted, as the need arose, to many regiments.

Of the Battalion proper, headquarters, first line transport and a small cadre, alone remained. Blossoming under the title of " Battalion Training Staff and Transport," this cadre marched to Bours. Bours proved to be a pleasant enough little village inhabited by friendly folk and well stocked with *vins, blanc et rouge,* to say nothing (the less said the better) of *bière anglaise.* Need it be remarked that with transport greater than personnel, the march there was taken in comfort, minus packs and steel hats ? The 28 miles was divided evenly by a halt at Blessy for a night.

Four days afterwards the four company commanders and Quartermaster were ordered to Auchel to join the 11th Garrison Guard Battalion Royal Scottish Fusiliers, for instructional purposes. A few days later one officer was sent to the 2nd (G.G.) Battalion Royal Irish Regiment at Hurionville on the same duty.

N

These battalions were made up of " B " and " C " Class men, who, unfit for active service, had been hurried out under the stress of events, to dig defensive positions in rear, in case of need.

Meanwhile the transport under Lieutenant H. A. Spendlove had left the cadre for the concentration camp at Etaples ; only the officers' chargers and a few limbers remained on strength. Numbers were further diminished a few days later by the departure of Captain Naylor, one company-quartermaster sergeant (C.Q.M.S. Lane) and two instructors for the Divisional Lewis-gun school as staff. C.Q.M.S. Lane did not remain long and was soon back with the cadre.

Ordinary routine, broken by range-firing and inoculation, filled in the month for the remnant. May had opened with the Battalion strength at 25 officers and 738 other ranks. It closed with a cadre totalling 11 officers and 72 other ranks.

At the beginning of June (2nd) the Battalion left Bours by bus and were attached to the 49th Infantry Brigade 16th (Irish) Division at Preures. Five days later a further move was made to Humbert, but the same night saw the cadre back again in Preures. On the 10th, another move, this time a real one, took the 2/5th to Bezinghem where they were attached to the 47th Infantry Brigade.

In the week that followed the area was thoroughly mapped out as a training ground, and billets arranged for the 317th American Infantry Regiment, who detrained at Samer on the 16th. As the Americans moved in, the 16th (Irish) Division moved out. This Division went back to Boulogne *en route* for England to be made up to strength.

The 2/5th had played many parts ; it now commenced to play an entirely new and novel rôle : that of guide and friend to an American Regiment. It had been rehearsing its part for some weeks ; instructors rubbing up their drill, musketry and bombing. Schools commenced on the 18th and the cadre was divided for general super-

vision among the several American battalions as follows :
Headquarters attached to Headquarters 317th Infantry Regiment.

" D " Company attached to 1st Battalion 317th Infantry Regiment.

" B " Company attached to 2nd Battalion 317th Infantry Regiment.

" C " Company attached to 3rd Battalion 317th Infantry Regiment.

" A " Company attached to Headquarters Company 317th Infantry Regiment.

By the 20th instruction was in full swing. Captain Drysdale, M.C., took charge of the Lewis-gun course and eight N.C.O. instructors were detailed to each battalion. Also twelve N.C.O.'s per battalion instructed in bombing under the general direction of Lieut. Lewis. Our instructors had as holidays, Sundays and such days as the Americans did tactical schemes.

The weeks spent thus, in close co-operation and work with the Americans, were thoroughly enjoyed by everybody. The Americans were keen and very eager to learn all our fellows had to teach them.

One story told by Captain Littleboy in his book is much too good and typical not to be quoted here :

A certain number of lectures were given, and amongst others, one by C.S.M. Robinson. The American Company Commander introduced him with words somewhat as follows : " Now here is a British Non. Com. who has come to talk to us this afternoon. He has fought in all of Britain's wars and has been out here since the beginning. I guess it will pay you to listen to what he says."

Interest in the British method of doing things was always lively, and the relative merits of our field-kitchens, limbers and equipment as compared with American were discussed among them at great length.

Although they were willing to accept our army way in a host of matters, they never forsook their beloved coffee for the subtle delights of well-mashed tea. Nor did they take too kindly to cricket, but preferred to spend their evenings playing their own national game of baseball.

On the 29th the Americans were reviewed by H.R.H. the Duke of Connaught, and six days later they left Bezinghem for active participation in the great struggle.

With their departure the 2/5th Training Cadre was out of a job. July was a most glorious month, and the whole of it was spent in a most enjoyable fashion by the Cadre. Living from day to day, hardly dreaming that such wonderful luck could last them for long, the mornings were occupied with ordinary training, and the afternoons and evenings were filled with cricket, river bathing, running, rifle competitions, walking, basket-ball, and baseball with the set left behind them by the Americans.

Of the many cricket matches played against neigh-bouring units only one was lost.

All sorts of rumours were afloat as to the disposal of the Cadre. These altered and grew as the month wore on. Finally at the beginning of August definite orders arrived.

The Cadre was disbanded on August 3rd.

The horses and transport were handed over to the 39th Divisional Train, care of the Area Commandant, Samer. The Commanding Officer proceeded to the C.O's " pool " at Etaples, the Quartermaster to the Quartermaster's " pool " at Calais, and the remainder to the 1/5th Battalion, the Sherwood Foresters.

As the few, who shared its identity and had helped to make its record and traditions, melted away on this quiet August night, this history properly comes to an end. Thus, without fuss or fanfare, the 2/5th Sherwood Foresters, which had endured as a separate entity through the storm of nearly four stressful years, dissolved into nothingness and became one with the mighty past.

CHAPTER XI

THE REMNANT

This said, they both betook them several wayes,
Both to destroy, or unimmortal make
All kinds ; and for destruction to mature
Sooner or later.

—MILTON, *Paradise Lost.*

ON August 6th the 2/5th Battalion Cadre joined the 1/5th
Battalion The Sherwood Foresters at Verquin.

Much as they would have liked it, Lieut.-Colonel A.
Hacking, M.C., found it impossible to keep them together
in one company, and they were allotted to the various
companies according to vacancies. But the old 2/5th
atmosphere and *esprit de corps*, to some extent, survived,
and its own 2/5th men went forward to even greater
glory and renown in the ranks of the 46th Division.

Therefore it is felt that something, however brief,
should be placed on record here to round off the heroic
tale and carry the adventures of the gallant remnant
down to the end, although the chronicler realizes he is
trespassing on ground that may possibly be dealt with
in another book by the historian of the 1/5th Battalion.

On August 8th, a date that will be ever memorable as
the day when the British offensive at Villers-Brettoneux
began, and the fortunes of war finally turned against the
Germans, the Remnant moved up as an integral part of
the 5th Battalion to the relief of the 5th Leicesters in the
Gorre sector. Four days later they were relieved by the
8th Sherwoods and went back to the Liverpool line just
in front of Gorre Wood. On the 14th they moved again
to the Essars sector near La Motte Farm.

Late at night on August 20th the expected German
retirement was reported, and at dawn the following

morning the forward companies advanced. The enemy had not, however, retreated very far, and after filling a gap in the forward line near Le Touret the Battalion was relieved and trekked back to Vaudricourt Wood. Major R. S. Pratt, M.C., afterwards received a well earned bar to his M.C., for his share in this day's operations.

On August 26th they were back in the line again in the neighbourhood of Sloane Square and the Rue de Bois. The Germans chose this time for another small retirement and the platoons spent the last days of the month in dodging forward from dyke to breastwork and from breastwork to dyke.

The 31st of this month saw them back in Gorre, billeted in the brewery cellars, where bathing in the La Bassée Canal was made possible.

Back again in the line near Richebourg Avoué the Battalion found itself squeezed out of the narrowing front and went back into Divisional rest (the first night of which was spent in cubicles in the Girls' School at Bethune) at Lahoussoye.

There in barns and billets the Battalion rested and trained and marched (G.O.C. Division, Major-General Boyd, believed in marching as an aid to fitness) till September 18th, when the whole Brigade were taken by lorry to Poeuilly quite close to Vraignes and Vermand, familiar ground to the 2/5th men. This long run through the night across the devastated area, lying silent, deserted and ghostly under the soft beams of a full moon, was an experience many will not forget. It was as if the magic story of seeming wasted endeavour, youthful hopes for ever blasted, countless tears shed and sorrows endured arose to mock these men who still survived and dared to traverse the brooding solitude of the scene.

At 5 a.m. on September 24th, "C" Company, assisted by Mr. Crellin's platoon ("A" Company), attacked Pontruet. The barrage put down was a very poor one and scarcely touched the German posts in and about Gallichet Alley. A tank made a timely appearance and helped to clear some of the machine-gun nests. The Lincolns and Leicesters had, meanwhile, penetrated the northern part of Pontruet, but the village proper had not been properly mopped-up and the enemy still held strong machine-gun posts.

In this fateful side-show the old 2/5th lost some of its very best men, including gallant Sergeant R. H. Ford, D.C.M., M.M., who took his men forward in rushes right up to the enemy wire. Spotting an enemy machine-gun post about 40 yards away, he got up and rushed towards it, hoping to find a gap in the wire through which he could reach it. He was met by a hail of bullets and was killed instantaneously.

That night the ground upon the hill top, looking down into the village, was consolidated, and just before dawn on the 25th the whole Battalion was relieved by the 8th and went back to a hot meal provided in Cookers Quarry.

Four days later (September 29th) occurred the attack which will rank for ever as a unique and stupendous achievement in a war full of new and unexpected things. On this day, under cover of a thick mist, the 46th Division forced the passage of the St. Quentin Canal and exploited that success to the depth of several miles.

The full story of that Deathless Day has already been fully told. Suffice it to record here that the remnant of the 2/5th, merged into its elder Battalion, fulfilled the share allotted it in the splendour of this event. Amongst those unfortunately wounded in this attack was Captain J. N. Jacques, M.C., the gallant Commander of " D " Company 2/5th at Mount Kemmel.

At five in the afternoon the Battalion had reached their objective, the Green line, 500 yards east of Lehaucourt, after an advance of five miles. At dusk, and according to plan, the 32nd Division leap-frogged the Green and went on to the Red line near Levergies.

Events during these last weeks moved quickly. The enemy was given no peace—no time to reorganize or prepare defences. Stroke after stroke was dealt him and their cumulative effect was to beat him to his knees.

On October the 3rd, at six hours' notice, the Battalion was once more in the thick of things at Ramicourt and Montbrehain.

The 5th Battalion on the right and the 8th on the left, in conjunction with the Anzacs and Staffords, were to attack these two villages on a narrow front of 2,000 yards. Tanks would assist.

In this engagement the enemy fought stubbornly, threw in reserves, and altogether gave the Battalion anything but a walk over. The Beaurevoir trench system was broken, but Ramicourt and Montbrehain were the scene of very desperate fighting. Both places were taken, but Montbrehain was recaptured by the enemy later in the day. The Commanding Officer was wounded early in the morning, and Major Pratt, M.C., took over command. During this engagement some troops on the right showed signs of weakening in their resistance and threatened thereby to leave the flank of the Battalion exposed.

Captain Littleboy, totally regardless of his own personal safety, visited them in an endeavour to stiffen their resistance. Immediately afterwards he was severely wounded by a bullet through the stomach. Of the decorations won this day four fell to " C " Company, Captain Littleboy being awarded a bar to his M.C. On this day, too, the Battalion received the highest honour a Battalion can receive. Sergeant W. H. Johnson of " B " Company was awarded the V.C. for most conspicuous gallantry and devotion to duty. Single-handed, he rushed two machine-gun posts, the second one in a severely wounded condition. But, unluckily, the success of this day was marred by the death of some very brave fellows. Amongst them must be mentioned Lieut. M. D. Barrows, who had been awarded an M.C. on the 21st September for very gallantly beating off a German attack.

The following fortnight was filled with a tour of duty in the line near Sequehart, being squeezed out on the 9th, a one day's rest at Levergies (hot baths and clean

clothes, oh joy!), a day at Mericourt, another at Fresnoy,
and finally (on the 13th) Bohain, where preparations
went forward for the coming attack on the Bohain-
Le Cateau line, in which the 5th were to have a
share.

This was to be a big thing. Five divisions were to
participate, and their job would be to make another big
salient in the enemy line and thus, once again, force
back his flanks.

At 5.20 a.m. on October 17th, the attack was launched.
The 5th operated in the neighbourhood of Guyot Farm,
towards Regnicourt. The attack was a complete success
—the Battalion, after fierce fighting and regrettable losses
from machine-gun fire, reached its objectives. Major
Pratt received and thoroughly earned a second bar to his
M.C. for his work in this attack.

That night it was relieved by the 6th Sherwoods and
went back to Fresnoy-le-Grand via Guyot Farm and
Bohain.

The Battalion stayed ten days in Fresnoy.

On October 29th, it began to trek towards the line once
more. The enemy was still continually on the move
backwards.

On November 5th, the Battalion came into touch again
with him at Prisches. The Germans were still in possession of the village; the 6th Sherwoods were just west of it,
the 5th one mile to their rear.

The next day the 5th were to carry the village in force,
drive the enemy out, and go on, if possible, as far as the
Green line, 3 kilos. east of Cartignies. Nearing Prisches,
as day broke, our men were met by excited civilians from
the outlying houses who reported the village evacuated
one hour before; a thorough search of every house and
cellar confirmed the news.

Reaching Cartignies in the early afternoon the
Battalion again found itself in close touch with the foe.
Entrenched in houses on the further bank of the Petite
Helpe river (then in flood) it was found impossible to
dislodge him by an immediate frontal attack, so the men,

worn out by the day's advance over heavy country, dug themselves in along the railway embankment.

As expected, the following morning found the Germans gone ; the river was bridged and the town entered without opposition.

This was the Remnant's last brush with the enemy.

Four days later, at eleven on the eleventh of the eleventh, the Armistice was signed, and, after four years of war, fighting ceased.

On November the 12th the Battalion moved from Cartignies to Boulogne-sur-Helpe ; to Landrecies on the 23rd ; to Beaurepaire on January 5th, 1919, thence to Bethencourt near Caudry and Cambrai.   Here demobilization was completed and the Cadre left for England on June 17th.

CHAPTER XII

Men that are men again, who goes home ?
Tocsin and trumpeter ! Who goes home ?
For there's blood on the field and blood on the foam.
And blood on the body when Man goes home.
  And a voice valedictory. . . . Who is for Victory ?
Who is for Liberty ? Who goes Home ?

G. K. CHESTERTON, *The Flying Inn.*

THUS, in small groups, unobtrusively, even as they had entered, our modest heroes leave the Lists. Dribbling back into civil life, they are picking up once more the threads of the old routine and are now, to all appearances, lost in the multitude of their fellows. Our stage is empty ; the story of their share in the war is finished. Remains only the Epilogue.

The years of the Great War were heavily charged with a wealth of sacrifice and suffering, profoundly affecting the lives of millions of human beings.

But what, it may be asked, has the soldier gained from out the wrack and turmoil of that bitter time ? Has he gleaned nothing beyond the consciousness of a part well played, a duty worthily accomplished, a victory measured in miles ?

Yes, consciously to many, and as a force working instinctively through others, has come a stronger and a surer grip upon their manhood.

From an inferno of terrors, more horrible than any imaginative novelist before the war dared place a man and keep him sane, the soldier emerges self-reliant, disciplined and alert. Tried in the crucible of war he has come forth, clothed, with respect for himself, and a new pride in his race. He now judges men and things

189

in the light of a new knowledge and a fresh experience
that augurs well for the future of our Empire.

Men have learned to appreciate at their true worth the
simple and abiding things of life—homes and garden,
flowers, wives and children ; to appraise their fellows,
not by what they appear to be, but by what they *really
are* ; to understand something of the ways of people
living in other parts of the world ; above all, they have
experienced with men from every social rank the comradeship that comes from dangers and discomforts
mutually shared.

We now know our own beloved Battalion to have been
especially rich both in splendid material and in that
intangible something called *esprit de corps*. Looking
back, two men (one an officer and one a ranker) stand
out pre-eminently as embodying in themselves all
that the Battalion stood for.   There were others.
But of these two, both alas ! dead, we can speak
freely.

Captain A. C. Judd, M.C., joined the Brigade as Church
of England chaplain whilst in England, and was attached
to the 2/5th both in Ireland and Overseas until the
fateful 21st March, 1918.

Padres were ever a mixed lot, but in Judd the Battalion
discovered a man after its own heart.

He was all that a Padre should be and a little more
besides.   He influenced us all tremendously.   Yet he
had few of those outward accomplishments that attract.
He did not play games ; he had no cheery hail-fellow-
well-met manner ; no fund of witty stories.   He was
pale, thin, shy and retiring.   But we knew him for what
he was—a saint among parsons and a man among men.
We trusted him.

One noticed his hands.   They were long and slender
and never still.   With them he filled in and expressed
all that he had to say.   He had, too, a nervous habit of
passing them from front to back across his unruly hair.

He was a colossal fidget.   His fingers played unconsciously and unceasingly with anything within reach.

He had a genius for untidiness, and spread his belongings behind him everywhere like a paper-chase.

But he never missed a tour of duty in the trenches. In his old tin-hat, with its fringe of frayed sandbag, box-respirator, more or less at the alert (rather less than more), and a stick, his pocket stuffed with chocolates and cigar-ettes, he would spend long, cold, wet nights wandering from sap to sap and from post to post, chatting to and hearten-ing the men in their weary vigil. Many times he came within an ace of being shot by our own men through his habit of wandering off without notice into No Man's Land in search of dead to bury.

He never knew the time. He would happen into the company dug-out at any odd hour with the mild inquiry, " Have I just missed a meal, or is there one coming ? " And if there was jam, his simple glee was a pleasure to watch. He *loved* jam.

He always went *over* with the Battalion, although he could have stopped comfortably behind in the transport lines without any dereliction from duty.

At Passchendaele he did heroic work amid the barrage, comforting and helping the men, binding up wounded and helping to take them back. Moving about among the shell-bursts, he was frequently thought to have been killed, but, half buried and choking from smoke, he survived. He seemed to bear a charmed life. For his work during this attack he was awarded the M.C.

The secret of his power lay, perhaps, not so much in his fearlessness nor in his unassuming modesty, nor yet in his willingness to serve even the least. It sprang from his profound understanding of, and sympathy with, the troubles of the ordinary human man.

He never preached. On church parade, with the men grouped around him in a hollow square, amidst the rum-ble of the guns and the nearer rattle of transport on the road, he would walk up and down before the piled drums and just talk to us quite simply about home, about life and about God. His attitude towards war was not the official attitude of a bishop. His views followed more closely the teachings of his Great Leader.

He never pandered to the newspapers, or pretended with them that Tommy enjoyed the war. In spite of the justice of the allied cause, his spirit was so attuned to, and weighed down by, the suffering of it all, that, at times, he must have prayed that under Divine Providence the agony should cease. In some subtle way we sensed this attitude of his. Perhaps this was the great secret of his hold over us.

In the debacle at Bullecourt in March, 1918, he shared for the last time the fate of the Battalion. Mortally wounded, he was taken prisoner and died soon after in German hands.

As one man said of him, and he would have wished for no finer epitaph, " He was a sky-pilot, but he was a *man* and a damned good sort."

Sergeant R. H. Ford, D.C.M., M.M., of " C " Company, possessed the same dauntless spirit as Captain Judd and had the same quiet retiring ways with him. Commencing as a private in the early days of the Battalion, he rose slowly through sheer merit and devotion to duty. Had he lived, he would undoubtedly have gone a great deal further up the ladder of promotion,* though in heroic disregard for his own personal safety when the lives of his men were at stake, he had no further heights to climb.

His small body enclosed a heart in which the straightforward simplicity of a child was combined with the bravery of a lion. Meticulously careful in his personal appearance, he came out of the trenches as spruce as he went in, his clear eyes twinkling in a fashion friendly to all the world.

His death at Pontruet was a sad blow to all who knew him. His Company Commander, Captain Littleboy, especially, felt his loss keenly. Writing of him in *The Battles of the Hundred Days*, he says : " Sergeant Ford

*Major Pratt remarked to a brother officer one day after Ford was killed, " I will always regret that we did not apply for Ford to be given the King's Commission on the battlefield."

and I were together the whole time we were in France, and I had never known him fail. Memories of Ford crowd in on me as I write—how at Ypres he went on firing his Lewis-gun during the Boche counter-attack, long after he was hit ; how at Mount Kemmel he covered the withdrawal of his company with his platoon, on three occasions, amidst very heavy shelling; and how he used to go out on patrols by himself, ' just to find out what the Boche was doing.' "

During the attack on September 24th, 1918, finding himself and No. 9 Platoon close up to the enemy wire and with a machine-gun only 40 yards away, he calmly and deliberately got up in an endeavour to find a gap through the wire and to rush the post single-handed.

Thus died Reggie Ford, as Captain Littleboy says : " the bravest little fellow we ever knew."

It was the example and devotion of men like Ford and Judd, typical of many others whom it is impossible to mention, which raised a battalion tradition second to none.

The long sojourn in England, the expedition to Ireland, followed by another long wait, all tended to lower the *morale* and the self-respect of the Unit. It began to feel that perhaps it wasn't *good enough* for real active service. Unluckily too, its arrival in the war zone coincided with the first German retreat, and its first failures were due, like its prolonged stay at home, to no fault of its own.

At Passchendaele it found itself at last, and from that time onward to the end of the war it never looked back.

The spirit of the men was extraordinary. In the tightest corner they could joke ; on their way to the grimmest of tasks they could sing.

It was this phlegmatic, not-worrying, what-a-joke outlook, mixed with dogged pluck, endurance and don't-know-when-I'm-beaten attitude that carried the Empire's soldiers through to Victory.

And so we leave them, drawing the curtain upon that

Epic Time. No doubt as the years pass memories will grow vague and many fade into forgetfulness ; even as the northern provinces of France will heal their scarred breasts and once more become beautiful and fruitful around the scattered graves of our fallen.

Yet out of all that agony of blood and sweat shall be born that new spirit of Liberty for which we fought and of which since the dawn of time mankind has dreamed.

POST SCRIPTUM

Whilst this book was being prepared for publication, Captain C. N. Littleboy and the Author spent two weeks of the summer of 1920 revisiting the war zone in France and Flanders.

Taking bicycles they saw once more most of the places mentioned in this History.

They visited Samer, Bezinghem, St. Omer, Cassel, Winnezeele, Poperinghe, Ypres, and the ground traversed by the Battalion in the operations before Passchendaele as described in Chapter VI. Afterwards, they turned south through Avion and Lens, Bullecourt and Ecoust to Albert. From there, moving east, Le Verguier, The Quarries, Flesquières and other places like St. Quentin and Peronne were visited.

The following brief account of their general impressions is given in the hope that it may prove interesting to some at least of their one-time comrades-in-arms.

Standing outside Albert railway station at 11 o'clock at night we searched the darkness for a gleam of light that might indicate a human habitation. Far away, growing fainter each moment, the Arras train clattered on its way to Bapaume, whilst the rain dripped steadily upon the dimly outlined ruins. Here, anyway, the British Soldier's France had not changed and we might be just arriving back off leave. . . .

Yet the war zone *has* changed and changed profoundly.

To the returning soldier the familiar places now seem foreign and strange. To him Northern France has suddenly become cold, desolate and empty.

Khaki no longer jostles good-humouredly along the streets, estaminets no longer ring to the hilarious shouts of British Tommies, lorries and limbers no longer rattle across the cobbles of the quaint squares of St. Omer. Towns like St. Pol, Doullens and Hazebrouck, which in time of war blossomed into busy marts, are, to-day, shrunk again to pre-war quietness.

And further up, in the devastated areas proper, the difference is even more noticeable. On roads once heavily congested by guns and transport it is possible to go for miles without meeting a soul. Lonely camps are everywhere veritable tragedies of decay ; huts with their windows gone, their doors sagging and their duck-board paths and horse lines lost beneath an upcrop of grass and weeds.

Amongst all this, in small groups scattered over wide districts, live the Burial Officers and their staffs, busy slowly collecting into large cemeteries the dead left buried where they fell across the battlefields.

For the most part the battlefields are still as our men last saw them, but for an overgrowth of grass, thistles, and wild flowers which hide from view shattered trenches and rusty wire. However, the French peasants, with wonderful courage and cheerfulness, have begun to make their land arable again by filling in shell-holes—a heart-less task in places like Riencourt and Souchez.

Bungalow villages have sprung up in localities one never thought to see them : a tiny colony of huts stands on Abraham Heights, weaving looms are at work in Villeret, peasant children now play in the Quarries, harvesting goes forward by Tiger Trench and a train steams to-day down Bunhill Row. Yet these sights in the battle zone are few and far between, though nearly every ruined village boasts of wooden huts, either complete or nearly so.

Passchendaele is almost unredeemed except for an estaminet and a few huts round the cross-roads at Wieltje. Otto and Somme Farms and other pill-boxes still stand, and the surrounding ground is still littered with shells, equipment, ground sheets and rusty rifles.

Ypres itself has become a mushroom city of hotels,

brightly painted structures clustering round the Menin
Gate and out along the road to Hooge. All day long
motor-cars and char-a-bancs dash into the Square in
front of the ruined Cloth Hall and disgorge their loads of
trippers. Early each week-day morning strings of lorries
bring workmen from Poperinghe who are busy clearing
away the debris of bricks and rubbish which at present
overlay the foundations of the city's one-time beauty.
Back on the Vlamertinghe road the metamorphosis is
complete. Everywhere the hutted camps, that once
lined that tragic road, have given place to cultivated
fields and trim bungalows.

Reminders of the British occupation are still much in
evidence from old weather-stained " Notices to Troops "
nailed to trees beside the roadways, to mugs, mess-tins
and even Colgate shaving-stick cases hanging on cottage
walls or standing, brightly polished, on mantelpiece or
bracket.

At some old billets one found oneself completely
forgotten, whilst at others, where least expected, one was
joyfully remembered and treated royally to *café avec
cognac* amid an embarrassing circle of wide-eyed children.

To revisit the scenes of those eventful years is a
saddening business. For, after all, only the husk remains. The France and Flanders we knew, and somehow loved in spite of all, has vanished. It disappeared
with the British Army.

THE GREEN TRIANGLE

www.ingramcontent.com/pod-product-compliance
Lightning Source LLC
Chambersburg PA
CBHW031952080426
42735CB00007B/360